Joyful in Hope

'Jean Gibson has an extraordinary ability to draw us into the lives of the women whose stories she tells. I was completely absorbed, touched and challenged by the way they not only came to terms with a host of difficult situations, but faced them with courage, dignity and hope. This book is indeed a treasure trove of surprising joy in unexpected places.'

Michele Guinness, author and speaker

'In his letter to the believers in Ephesus in Ephesians 2:10, the Apostle Paul wrote, "For we are God's workmanship, created in Christ Jesus to do good works, which God prepared in advance for us to do." As Jean traces the story of one courageous woman's life after another, she invites us to wonder at the beauty of God's workmanship which shapes lives that, in the midst of the brokenness of our world, shine with his goodness. Read and be inspired to "run with perseverance the race that is set before us".'

Mike Treneer, International President, The Navigators

'Each of these personal stories, told so vividly by Jean, drew me again into the wonder of our God who is at work in the intimate details of our lives. Our life journeys are times of graced light and graced darkness. Jean's book reminds us we live bathed in grace, and it is this that enables us to indeed live "joyfully in hope".'

Sally Longley, retreat leader, spiritual director and honorary associate minister, Sydney, Australia

'Encouraged and excited is the way that *Joyful in Hope* has imprinted my life. As I followed their lives and stories of the eight women I was encouraged by their faithfulness and hope in Jesus as they faced very difficult family and sometimes life-threatening situations. I was gripped by the sensitive way each story has been written and felt a bond with these people. I was continually reminded that when we become Christians God promises to be with us in all situations. He never promises, however, to remove the trials of the world. In spite of the difficulties faced these people have always felt God standing beside them every step of the way, pouring compassion on them even in very dark hours (Psalm 103:13). I found it difficult to put the book down and saw it as a great encouragement for my Christian walk.'

Julie F. Mathews, Head of Education, Wesley Institute,
New South Wales, Australia

'This book is a story of real women living real lives. It shows us that there is hope in the midst of despair and that God *does* give inner strength to cope with life's tragedies. It is a reminder that faith in God is the greatest hope we have – here we see the reality of women whose living faith in Jesus carries them through. Women everywhere will draw much strength and encouragement from this book.'

Caroline Hawthorne, General Secretary, Presbyterian Women

'An accident, illness or trauma can change our lives in a moment. How would *you* cope? We are indebted to the individuals who have been willing to be vulnerable and share their warts and all stories in *Joyful in Hope*. Jean Gibson's gift of sensitively documenting these accounts brings hope to all of us that God's grace and comfort takes many forms.'

John Brown, Operation Mobilisation

Joyful
in Hope

Finding God in the Extremes

Jean Gibson

Authentic

British Library Cataloguing in Publication Data

A catalogue record for this book is available from the British Library

ISBN 978-1-86024-808-5

Cover design by Paul Airy (www.designleft.co.uk)
Printed and bound in Great Britain by Bell and Bain, Glasgow

To Karen

A joyful smile
A loving heart
An enduring faith

Contents

Acknowledgements

It is not always easy to be vulnerable and open about our feelings when life is tough and we are at our lowest point. Yet the power of this book is that the women in it have been willing to do just that. I am immensely grateful for their courage and co-operation throughout the writing process. Without it, the book would not have happened. Thank you to all of you – it is your book.

My heartfelt thanks also go to Malcolm Down, Liz Williams and all at Authentic Media, with whom it has again been a pleasure to work. I am grateful to a number of friends who kindly agreed to read parts of the manuscript and especially to Carolyn Gowdy who read it in its entirety, offered helpful suggestions and supplied the constant encouragement that every writer needs.

Brian, thank you for your patience, your acts of kindness, your steadfast love. You are the base from which I operate. Thank you to Andrew (especially for the website), Peter, both Sarah Janes, Samuel and Nathanael for reminding me constantly of the precious gift of family and for the joy you bring to my life. You help me to be Joyful in Hope.

Introduction

Since the publication of *Seasons of Womanhood*, I have been overwhelmed by the stories that have come back to me, of lives touched and spirits lifted as people realised they were not alone in their situation.

For that reason, I have produced this second volume of stories, in similar format – stories of women of all ages, facing challenges that many of us encounter in some form or other. As before, all the stories are true, although occasionally names have been changed to protect identities.

If your faith is stronger and clearer as a result of reading this book, then it will have been worthwhile. I would be very interested to hear your story also. You can contact me through my website www.jeangibson.co.uk and read other stories there.

1

Second Chance

Fluttering white streamers, bright in the sunshine, the waves blew across the sea towards the quiet beach. A small yacht moved silently along the horizon, sails catching some invisible wind. Seagulls swooped and called as the sky cleared, cloud dissipating in the brilliance of the sun and the fresh cleanness of a new day.

Louise and Colleen stood at the edge of the car park, surveying the bay. The surf looked good and it seemed a perfect day to try out the new bodyboards which Colleen had acquired the previous week. The beaches on the picturesque north coast of Ireland were always popular with surfers, but this early in the day there were few people about. The April weather did not encourage anyone to sit on the beach but the occasional jogger and dog-walker made their way purposefully along the hard sand near the water's edge. Clutching their boards, the sisters ran down the beach in their wetsuits and splashed joyously into the water.

Having finished her studies the year before, Louise had recently found her dream job with a mission agency working in Africa. Her interest in that country had begun years earlier when she spent some weeks on a summer team in Kenya, helping to renovate a nursery school and interacting with the children there through music and sport. The experience had opened her eyes to the situation in Kenya and given her a love for the children, who were so hungry for education and attention.

A year later, sponsored by the Church Mission Society, she returned to a short-term post in the Kenyan nursery school she had renovated with the team. Six months working as an assistant teacher gave her the opportunity to test more fully the sense of calling she had felt on her previous visit. She came back to Ireland knowing that her future would in some way be linked with Africa. A three-year course in early childhood studies at teacher training college in Belfast seemed a sensible option but, that completed, she paused to consider the next step. What did God want her to do?

A job advertised locally in an organisation called Fields of Life, with links in East Africa, seemed to be the answer to her prayers. She was appointed as volunteer co-ordinator, preparing teams from churches and youth groups to go to Uganda during the summer. Meeting regularly with them to work on team building, cultural orientation and spiritual preparation, she also worked with volunteers who supported the work in Ireland. In March 2008, Louise travelled to Burundi, Rwanda and Uganda, observing the Fields of Life work for herself. She loved what the organisation was doing, making a difference to children in Africa through education, helping people to help themselves. She was fulfilled in her job and thrilled to feel that she had finally identified the role God had for her.

On that April morning, Louise was relaxed and carefree, content in the shape her life was taking, looking forward to a fun day out with her sister. As they entered the water, she revelled in the strong waves knocking her back as she waded out into the sea. Conditions were perfect for bodyboarding. At first they surfed happily together near the shore, until Colleen decided to venture further out to catch the waves before they broke and get a longer surf back in. Both sisters were confident swimmers and loved the water, but Louise was happy to stay closer to the shore, allowing the waves to pick her up and take her with them to the beach. She forgot about time, luxuriating in the adrenaline-charged rush of water carrying her forward.

Some time later, looking around to get her bearings, she realised that Colleen was moving further out from the shore without coming in on the waves. Wondering what she was doing, Louise called out to her.

'Are you OK?'

'Yes, I'm fine,' shouted Colleen.

Content that all was well, Louise turned her attention back to her board and concentrated on catching the next good wave.

It was a giant one. As the wave approached, Louise was poised and ready. This was going to be great! She lifted herself up onto the crest of the wave, but as it broke, instead of being swept forward, she felt herself being pulled back, off the board and down under the water. The board was still attached to her wrist, but as she surfaced again she thought, 'That's strange, I can't touch the ground. I thought that wave would have carried me in to the shore.' Unconcerned, she swam and surfed towards the beach. After a few minutes, however, she realised that however hard she swam, or tried to surf on the board, she was making no progress – in fact the shore seemed to be receding as she watched.

The realisation dawned that she was caught in a rip current that was carrying her out from the shore. It had never happened to her before, but she remembered what she had been taught in the past – she should not fight it, but swim along parallel to the shore until she got out of it. Determined not to panic, she took note of a landmark on the beach and set off swimming along the shore. When she checked again, however, she seemed to have made no progress. Realising she would have to try harder, she redoubled her efforts, trying to swim more strongly. She looked back at the shore again – still no further along. She was now the same distance out to sea as Colleen.

She began alternately swimming as hard as she could and stopping to tread water while she caught her breath. The next time she paused, it was with the gripping realisation that she was further from the shore than Colleen and would soon be far away from her. Quickly she called out to her, 'I'm stuck in a rip current here!'

Colleen managed to swim to her. 'I was caught in a rip before when you called to me,' she admitted. 'Let's swim together in that direction and really go for it to get out of this current.'

Together the sisters launched out again, confident in their ability to escape the pull of the tide that was carrying them steadily from the shore.

After a few minutes, however, Louise stopped to get her breath back. She realised she was tiring and could only swim for short periods without stopping to rest. Although the body-board was still attached to her wrist and she was able to use it from time to time, it was not enough to support her full body weight, so the only way to get her breath back was by constantly stopping to tread water. Out of her depth and unable to rest, she could feel her strength fading. Side by side, the sisters fought their way through the choppy water.

Looking back at the beach, Louise realised it was even further away than before; they were being swept out to sea. She was now tiring quickly. Colleen, stronger and fitter than Louise, was drawing ahead of her in the water as Louise kept stopping to rest. 'Keep swimming!' shouted Colleen, but by this time Louise was totally exhausted and was finding it difficult to keep going. Colleen could tell things were bad. She kept turning round and shouting to Louise, 'Keep swimming. You can't give up.' Desperately Louise kept trying, but she was finding it difficult to get her breath and realised she was beginning to lose the battle.

'If you can make it – get back to the beach yourself – get help for me!' yelled Louise.

'No fear!' shouted Colleen. 'I'm not leaving you. Take a minute to get your breath back, then try again.' She turned and swam back to where Louise was now clinging frantically to her board.

Half supported by the bodyboard, desperately treading water, Louise tried to calm herself. Summoning up all her strength for one last try, she threw herself into the water again, swimming for all she was worth. In a few moments, she knew she was making no progress and could go no further.

'Swim! Don't stop!' shouted Colleen desperately. But Louise could do no more. Unable to breathe properly, swallowing water, she had no strength left.

She looked once more at the beach. It was so far away now, it seemed impossible that they would ever get back there. She glanced out to sea. There was nothing but water as far as she could see and she was being swept out into that vastness. As the truth came home to her, she started to shout and wave her arms. Even as she did it, she realised the waves were so high and so noisy, there was no chance that anyone could hear her. By now Colleen was yelling desperately, 'Stop shouting and keep swimming!'

Louise looked at the beach again. A small group of people seemed to be walking along the water's edge and a few were wandering around the car park beyond, but no one had paid any attention to her attempt to attract attention. Frantically she waved her hands again and screamed for all she was worth. Could they not see her?

It was no use, they were too far away to hear or see anything. Steadily the current was continuing to drag the sisters out to sea. As she looked at where they were heading, she realised how much trouble they were actually in.

In her head, she knew she needed to keep calm and not panic but in the face of her inexorable progress away from land towards the great emptiness of the sea and the ever-present pull downwards beneath the water, she could not help panic taking hold. She began taking short, sharp breaths, hyperventilating. She felt dizzy and sick. She longed to fill her lungs with air, but all she was taking in was water. Watching helplessly nearby, trying to keep afloat herself, Colleen kept screaming 'Swim! Don't give up! Don't give up!' As if from far away, Louise could hear her but through the mist of panic and exhaustion, somehow she was unable to register what Coleen was saying or to respond to her. Dimly she was aware of her inability to breathe, alongside the need to keep kicking her legs and to keep her head above water.

The understanding dawned that she had come to the end of her resources. She had run out of energy to keep going. Looking back at the beach, so far away now, where no one could see her, Louise realised, as if in slow motion, what was happening. She was growing weaker and feeling cold. She tried to fight off the terrifying thought but it was a reality – she was going to drown. This was it. A flow of questions began to pass through her mind. *How long will it take? What will it feel like? Will it hurt? Will I pass out first so I don't know what's happening? What will Colleen do if she watches me go underwater and drown? Will I be found later or will I be swept out to sea?*

As the thoughts floated through her mind one after the other, Louise gave up. She no longer cared what happened. Unable to tread water any longer or to pull herself up onto the board, unable even to feel her legs any more, she simply put her head down on the board, closed her eyes and waited for it to happen. With the swell coming over her face, she was unable to breathe. For some reason, only at that very late stage, as she rested her head on the board, did she think to pray.

'God, this is my last chance. You need to do something right now.'

Amongst all the fear, pain and exhaustion she suddenly experienced a few seconds of total peace. For a moment her whole body relaxed and went to the opposite end of the spectrum from the blind panic she had just known.

At that point she lifted her head one last time and looked at the shore. Dimly she saw a young man in blue jeans running down the beach from the car park, a surfboard under his arm. She wondered vaguely, *Could he be coming to help me? Is God answering my prayer? I'm so far out, will he get here in time? Will he be able to help Colleen too?* Waves of panic swept over her again, but now she fixed her eyes on the young man battling through the waves towards her on his surfboard. Suddenly he was right in front of her. He slipped off the board, put his hand on her shoulder and spoke words that were almost unbelievable.

'My name's Martin and I'm here to take you back to the shore,' he said.

Could it really be happening?

'I want you to take hold of one of my ankles when I lie on the surfboard. Now hold on tight.' With Colleen and Louise each holding desperately on to an ankle with both hands, Martin powered through the water on his board, parallel to the shore. It felt so wonderful to be moving purposefully with someone else in control. Another wave swept over Louise, however, and in her weak state, she could not keep her hold on the precious ankle. She slipped off under the waves again. Martin stopped to pick her up. Together Colleen and Martin managed to get her back to the surfboard. Colleen held on to Louise's wetsuit and between them they dragged her through the water.

Once out of the current, Martin headed in towards the shore until the water was shallow enough for them to walk.

Together, Martin and Colleen helped Louise stumble in the last few metres towards land. At one point she dropped to her knees and burst into tears. Together they lifted her up and half-carried her on to the beach.

The crew from the local lifeboat, which had suddenly appeared off-shore, came running over with a foil blanket and oxygen. Never would Louise forget that first great breath of pure oxygen, reviving and exhilarating.

The coastguard arrived in his jeep, piled Colleen and Louise on board and drove them quickly to the nearest hospital, five miles away. Once there, Louise submitted to all the usual tests after such an incident, including oxygen levels and chest X-rays. Secondary drowning, sometimes a complication of having taken water into the lungs, can be a possibility even several hours later, as fluid in the lungs impairs the breathing process. However, all seemed to be clear. Dazedly, Louise lay in the hospital and talked to the coastguard and Martin.

As they recounted the sequence of events from their perspective, she realised just what a miracle had taken place. Martin, a keen surfer, had known the surf was going to be good that day and arrived in the car park to check the waves and decide whether to surf there or somewhere else. Standing looking out to sea, he had spotted Louise and Colleen and realised they were in trouble. Immediately, he telephoned the coastguard for help and then, fully dressed, grabbed his surfboard and ran into the water.

As she listened, Louise had no doubt that God had intervened that day. It seemed almost as if he had waited until she gave up and cried out desperately to him for help. Martin turned out to be one of the country's top surfing instructors, with a surf school in the local town. He was exceptionally strong, fit and experienced, well able to cope with powerful tides and currents. Having been a lifeguard along that particular stretch of coast in the past, he knew the beach extremely well and understood all about rip currents and the best way of dealing with them. If she had put in a request for a specific person to come and save her, she could not have chosen better than Martin.

On arrival at the hospital, Louise's heart rate had been very high. After a few hours she was well enough to go home, but two days later was re-admitted with a raised heart rate and suffering from delayed shock. It was a number of weeks before her body recovered physically.

A few days after the event, the story appeared in the local newspaper. Louise contacted Martin, who later took her back into the ocean near where the incident had occurred and gave her a proper surfing lesson. He talked to her about the currents prevalent on the North Coast, how to spot them, how to avoid them and what to do if she was ever caught in one again. Louise knew she could never repay him, not just for saving her life, but for caring about the quality of that life he had given her back, taking time to help her face her fear of going back into the water and helping her recover her confidence.

Despite the therapeutic benefits of revisiting the scene of the incident, however, Louise found herself gripped by nightmares in the weeks that followed. She kept seeing herself in various scenarios where she was dying, not always drowning, but losing her life in different ways. She shared these nightly terrors with friends, who prayed very specifically for her protection and recovery. The nightmares persisted, but they began to change – the dreams generalised to other people dying as well as her.

For about six weeks she was pursued by a sense of dread, haunted by thoughts of death during the day and nightmares at night. She could not shake off the awareness of how close to death she had come. She began to wonder if she would ever recover from the trauma of the experience. Friends at work recommended a counselling service which they thought might help.

Deciding to try it, she took what courage she had in both hands and made her way to Belfast every Thursday afternoon during July and August. Gradually, she was able to talk through the events of that day as they had happened and verbalise how she had felt at the time. She found it especially difficult as she tried to put into words the sensation of surrendering her life – the point when, out in the open sea, unable to keep her head above water, she simply stopped struggling and gave up her will to live. The retelling of that moment when she faced the end of her life, brought a feeling of terror beyond belief. As she talked, however, she found that other issues came to the surface which she needed to address. In time, she was able to think and talk about the whole episode in a more rational way.

Talking also helped her realise what God had done. She was conscious of a significant difference in her attitude to life as she considered the second chance she had been given. Facing the end of her life had been a profound emotional experience that changed her fundamentally; it was almost as if she had become another person. Committed to following Christ before, she was now determined to use her life to make a difference in the world.

One day, three months later, she was sharing with a friend who was going through a difficult situation. As she related her own experience, the realisation suddenly came to her.

'We can go through difficult circumstances and feel we are drowning in our troubles and can't see any way out. We think no one sees or cares, but when we cry out to God, he will rescue and reach out to us. I really see God now as my rescuer. What happened to me physically has become a permanent, powerful reminder of how God can literally save us.'

At that time she read some verses that jumped out at her in their significance: 'He reached down from on high and took hold of me; he drew me out of deep waters' (Ps. 18:16). Later in that passage verse 19 says: 'He brought me out into a spacious place; he rescued me because he delighted in me.'

'That thought totally changed my outlook. To think that God delighted in me, brought me ten million times closer to him. Rather than seeing me as unlovely or as a failure or disappointment, he feels joy when he sees me – not because of anything I do or don't do, but because I am his child. I was also gripped by the realisation that if I had died that day, I would have died not having done a great deal for God. Now I had a whole new perspective on serving him. I identified completely with the psalmist in Psalm 40:8, "I desire to do your will, O my God". Living for him one hundred per cent meant so much more than it did before.'

How that would work out in her life was unclear, however. The financial downturn faced by many organisations and businesses across the United Kingdom in 2008 was also affecting charities. In September, Louise heard that the job she loved so much was coming to an end. She was devastated. What was God doing? She was filled with this new desire to serve him utterly, and the job she was in seemed the most suitable place to do that. How could God allow this opportunity to close for her just now? He knew she was still coming to terms with what had happened and he knew how much she wanted to serve him with all she had. Questions swirled ceaselessly in her mind.

As her date for leaving drew near, tortured by feelings of doubt, insecurity and confusion about the way ahead, she went along to the local Global Leadership Summit – a conference she had booked some months earlier, long before she had any idea that she would be rethinking her future when she attended. The significance of its content and timing would be more profound than she could have guessed.

'The event looked at issues such as surrendering completely to God, serving him, finding my passions and aligning with

God's passion, working out what he wanted to do with my life. I was shocked into stillness before him as I realised God was speaking to me clearly through all that had happened. He had a particular purpose for me. I had almost lost my life, but he had given it back to me for a reason. What I had to do was make sure I used this precious gift in the way he wanted.'

It was an opportunity for Louise to refocus. What was her passion? It had always been Africa. Africa and children. What did God want her to do with these twin passions he had placed in her heart? Suddenly the desolation at losing her job gave way to excitement as she realised that everything that had happened in recent months was part of God's plan. He had brought her dramatically to a point where she was totally committed to him and completely open to his plan for her. Although she had felt she was following God's way for her life before her near death experience, she could now identify in a new way with Paul in the Damascus road encounter that changed his life around. God had intervened in an unusual way to catch her attention. He certainly had it now! She was determined to stay close to him and be ready to act as soon as he showed her the way ahead.

In the first week after her job with Fields of Life came to an end, she was offered another – working with disabled young people. She could hardly believe she was being given the opportunity to work with children, to concentrate for a short time on one of her passions as she waited for God's plan to unfold more fully. In the weeks that followed, she talked to mature Christian friends about what she felt God was saying to her. She met with people from different organisations working in Africa and looked at the opportunities available. The more she talked and thought and prayed about it, the stronger the thought persisted: This is what I am called to do. Avidly she read about situations in Africa and wanted to apply to them all.

One possibility impressed itself upon her as particularly relevant. Youth With A Mission were running a Discipleship Training School in South Africa called 'Children in Need'. As she looked at it, Louise realised it would give her good training for more long-term work. It involved some months' training in South Africa, followed by practical outreach in Zimbabwe. The situation in Zimbabwe was uncertain and some questioned her choice.

'Are you crazy? Look at what's happening in Zimbabwe. Why would you think of going there?'

For a few days Louise was thrown into turmoil again: *Should I listen to these people? Is this God speaking or not?* Above all, she did not want to miss his plan. She sent a text to a trusted Christian friend, confiding her fears and uncertainties: 'Am I crazy?'

As she went to bed she opened her Bible and read Mark chapter nine, the familiar story of a father who brought his son to Jesus, saying, 'If you can do anything, please help.'

'What do you mean "if"?' was the basic content of Jesus' reply. 'There are no ifs among believers.'

'I do believe; help me overcome my unbelief,' was the father's response.

Louise lifted her heart to God in a fervent prayer for guidance. 'Lord, I believe you are guiding me; help me with my questions. If you are calling me to this Discipleship Training School, then please make it clear so I can go with an easy mind.'

Some time later she read on into Mark chapter ten: 'Take courage, stand up, he is calling you.' The blind man knew Jesus was there, but nothing happened until he stood up in response to Jesus' call. Louise's heart filled with peace. God had opened the way for her to do this training with children in Africa. He would sort out the details and bring her through whatever lay ahead. She sent off the application form.

As she looks ahead, there are still many unknowns, but Louise realises that God's plan will become clear as she follows step by step. She feels very privileged to have come through her experience in the sea off the Irish coast early in her life – it has altered her perspective for all the years to come. She faces the future with her heart set on living as close to God as she can, deepening her relationship with him, following his plan and living it out day by day as he makes it clear. And she still goes surfing sometimes!

He brought me out into a spacious place; he rescued me because he delighted in me.
Psalm 18:19

2

Biscuit Please Mummy

Rosie hummed softly as she accelerated out of the Friday rush-hour traffic into the fast lane of the motorway. The promise of a leisurely weekend of long walks and uninterrupted conversation had made Karen's invitation to the Fermanagh Lakes impossible to refuse. It would be the perfect antidote to a week in the classroom.

Two hours later she was looking questioningly at a dinner table set for four. Karen's husband she was prepared for, but another guest? 'Oh, the minister's coming too,' said Karen airily. 'I feel sorry for him living on his own so I thought we'd invite him to dinner.'

Despite Rosie's misgivings, Revd David Cupples turned out to be good company and the tentative friendship begun that weekend developed into a full-scale romance. A year after their first meeting in June, Rosie and David were preparing for a September wedding. As a teacher, a wedding during the school summer holidays would have been the sensible plan for Rosie but, with no idea that she would be planning a wedding, she had already agreed to lead a youth trip to India that summer. The wedding would have to wait until September.

Applying for a teaching post in the local convent school, Rosie made clear to the interviewing panel that not only was she not Roman Catholic, but she would also not be available for the month of September and part of October. They still offered her the job.

Married to the local Presbyterian minister and involved in youth work in the church, she appreciated this unique opportunity to live and work in two different worlds. Eleven people had died in the Enniskillen Remembrance Sunday explosion just seven years earlier and the Good Friday Agreement was still four years ahead, but there was a desire across the local community for reconciliation and peace. Rosie was aware of how privileged she was to be straddling the divide.

Two years later, life changed with the arrival of a new baby, although Ellen was accommodating from the outset and slept for eight hours every night. Disproving all forecasts, she continued to sleep contentedly through the night for the next six months until Rosie went back to work. With this perfectly behaved first baby well installed in the family, Rosie and David looked forward to having another.

Things were not quite so straightforward second time around however. Rosie had various gynaecological problems and began to worry that Ellen would be their only child. Four and a half years later she eventually found she was pregnant again, to the great delight of the whole family. Ellen, now at nursery school, was old enough to be excited too and was overjoyed at the prospect of having a brother or sister. The pregnancy proceeded smoothly, Peter was born in February 2001 and Rosie went back to work in June.

Peter was not a cherub as a baby, but for the family it was a very happy time. Although he was less compliant than Ellen, it seemed to Rosie a more normal situation, as she experienced the sleepless nights that were meant to go with motherhood. She was very glad that Ellen had a brother and was not the lonely child she had feared during the years before Peter's birth.

One Sunday morning, a month after Peter's second birthday, Rosie picked him up from crèche after church as usual. Her friend Sheila, who was helping in crèche that day, asked carefully, 'Have you ever thought that Peter might have developmental problems?' Taken aback, Rosie looked at her blankly. Sheila, with her medical background, was normally very sensitive in her comments.

'What do you mean?' Rosie was puzzled.

'He doesn't play with other children in the crèche or even seem aware that there are other children around.'

'Oh well,' said Rosie scooping him up, 'lots of folk in my family aren't sociable, so you would hardly expect him to be.'

Laughing it off, she said her goodbyes at church and shepherded the children to the car. She was not particularly worried about the comment, but she did relay the conversation to David on the way home. 'What do you think she could have meant?' she wondered aloud.

David said very little but when they arrived home he disappeared into the study while Rosie prepared lunch. A short time later he walked into the kitchen and wordlessly handed her a document he had printed out from the computer.

In growing alarm, she read the article *Five Early Signs of Autism*.[1] The article stated that all parents should consider these 'Big Five' if they suspect their child may have autism:

1. Does the child respond when his/her name is called?
2. Does the child engage in 'joint attention'? (e.g. draw your attention to something he/she finds interesting)
3. Does the child imitate others? (e.g. imitate sounds or facial movements)
4. Does the child respond emotionally to others? (e.g. smile at someone who smiles at them)
5. Does the child engage in 'pretend play'?

Rosie thought about Peter with his cars – all he did was arrange them in a line. If she handed him a toy cup and teapot he had no idea what to do with it.

In the one minute it took Rosie to read through the list, her world changed. She knew she was reading a description of Peter. If she had sat down to describe him, these were exactly the factors she would have highlighted. She didn't know that autism was a developmental disorder. She had no idea that 'developmental problems' meant something as serious as autism. When Sheila made the remark, Rosie had wondered whether she meant that perhaps he needed speech therapy because he was slow to talk. Suddenly she recognised all the signs that had passed her by until this moment. Stunned, she thought, *How can I have had my head in the sand to such an extent? How did I not see what was so obvious?*

Ellen had been talking in sentences at eighteen months – at his eighteen month check-up Peter only had two words: cah (car) and baw (ball). The health visitor had been reassuring, pointing out that boys were different from girls in their development and often slower to develop speech. She didn't seem to have any great concerns about Peter. Rosie had accepted her explanation at face value and applied it not just to Peter's speech, but to other differences in the development of the two children. Shocked, the realisation that this reassurance had been misplaced now flooded through her.

Rosie had been telling herself not to be an over-anxious parent, but now that she thought about it, Peter did not seem to understand language. Frantically she cast around for an alternative solution, telling herself, *This is only one person's comment; there could be other explanations for his behaviour.* Desperate to get a second opinion, hoping against hope, Rosie and David arranged an urgent appointment to see their doctor the following morning. Hesitantly, he agreed there might be a problem and referred Peter to a paediatrician. The two-week wait for that appointment was short, given the current waiting lists, but to Rosie it seemed to last forever.

When the day eventually came, the paediatrician was kind and friendly. After an hour's close observation of Peter, she looked straight at his anxious parents as she delivered her diagnosis: 'There is no doubt whatsoever. He has Autistic Spectrum Disorder.' As she heard the words 'There is no doubt', Rosie's hope died. In the days to come she would learn more about exactly what 'Autistic Spectrum Disorder' meant. For now her main awareness was the end of hope. Up to that point she had been trying to hold on to the thought that Peter's symptoms might point to something less awful than autism. As she walked blindly out of the paediatrician's room she realised they were all beginning a very different life from the one they had before.

Almost immediately, Rosie's body reacted by going into shock. She felt dazed and helpless, aware only of the hopelessness of the situation. What she already knew about autism was pretty grim. Her childminder's sister taught a beginners' class in the local autism unit, from which she often returned with bruises. She had once commented, 'To hear that your child has autism must be the worst news parents can get.' Now these words reverberated in Rosie's mind. Building on her limited experience, she pictured the worst case scenario – a lonely child endlessly rocking, banging his head, cut off from the rest of society. Apart from the impact on her and David, she was terrified of what the future might hold for Ellen – what had they landed her with? What would home life be like for her?

In the days immediately after the diagnosis, neither Rosie nor David could eat or sleep. Never having had a significant bereavement in her life, this was the greatest sense of loss Rosie had ever experienced. 'It was very black. I was aware of the loss of what I thought I had – all my hopes and dreams for my son. It was not that I wanted him to be anything outstanding, just a normal little boy. David, in particular, had been looking forward to playing football and pursuing all the usual adventurous activities a dad enjoys with his son. The realisation that we would never do most of these things with Peter was devastating.'

Two things kept Rosie going. In her early years as a Christian she had received good teaching and had strong spiritual roots that gave her stability in the crisis. She knew she had somewhere to turn when everything seemed catastrophic. Secondly, in that first week after the diagnosis, although surrounded by the blackness of despair, she and David felt closer than they had ever been before as they realised no one else in the world was affected in the same way they were by this tragedy. On the morning after they saw their doctor, Rosie took two days' leave from school. She and David went for a walk that afternoon and as they walked they shared Bible verses, reassuring each other that God would be with them and that nothing could happen without God allowing it. They laid good foundations that day for the months and years ahead.

A strong faith did not mean Rosie had no questions. She had been full of joy when Peter was born, after four and a half years of waiting, only to be crushed by this news of his disability. 'God knew Peter would have autism and I didn't. It seemed cruelly unfair to be allowed that happiness at his birth, only to be plunged into this nightmare. David and I felt it was important to be honest with one another and with God about our feelings in all this.'

They grieved very differently. Initially, David cried for two days, but then he seemed to put grief to one side, re-immerse himself in his church work, and cope by getting on with life. Rosie could not cry – she was in shock and tears did not come until much later. For her, coming to terms with the situation was a long, slow, painful process with a developing understanding of what it would mean.

During those initial traumatic days she felt she could not put food in her mouth. She was aware of a bizarre sensation of existing but not living. 'I have never experienced anything like it before or since. I was not able to eat or sleep. Friends who have been suddenly bereaved tell me they have had the same reaction.' A week after she heard the news, knowing she had to keep well herself if she was to look after the children, Rosie forced herself to take her first few bites of food.

It was difficult sharing the news with friends and family because most of them had been as oblivious to the problem as David and Rosie. Rosie's sister, who worked with children with special needs, may have privately suspected that something was not quite right. Her mother had occasionally said, 'There's something different about Peter.' Rosie had joked with her about all the odd people in the family and replied, 'How could he be anything else?' At that stage they knew little about autism and were totally unaware of the significance of Peter's behaviour. Looking back, Rosie now realises there were a number of signs in the early days that all was not well but at the time they did not seem significant. She is glad they had those two early, very happy years with, as they thought, two normal healthy children.

People around them found it difficult to understand what they were going through. 'Other people are in a worse position,' one friend said unhelpfully. Rosie did not risk replying. 'One person told me about her friend whose child was terminally ill with cancer. To be perfectly honest, at that stage I felt that a terminal diagnosis would be easier to deal with because at least it would be clear cut and I would know what I was facing. I didn't dare say it, but I was aware that Peter's autism was something I would have to live with for the rest of my life.

At that moment I felt autism was the worst thing that could happen to anyone. I needed people to stand with me in the situation rather than saying how much worse it could be.'

The practical support from church and friends was overwhelming, shown in a hundred ways, from cards to cakes. One note that Rosie will always remember said, 'I realise this does not change the situation in any way but I want to let you know we love you and are thinking about you.' These thoughtful gestures helped carry them through the early days of shock and hopelessness.

In the midst of her grief Rosie was overwhelmingly grateful to Sheila who had had the courage to speak to her about her suspicions of Peter's condition. With her medical background, she knew that the sooner Peter was diagnosed, the sooner he would get on to the inevitable waiting lists for help. Because Peter's diagnosis happened quite rapidly, Rosie realised they had been spared months of worry, wondering what the problem was. 'I would never choose to get a shock like that but in retrospect it was better than months of watching Peter's behavioural problems develop and wondering what we were doing wrong.'

When parents first receive a diagnosis of autism, they have no idea what it will mean, because every child is different and the condition affects everyone differently. The ways the disorder can affect an individual are very diverse and problems can vary greatly from one child to another. Not in any state to be proactive herself, Rosie was grateful to friends who gave her books about other families with autism, books that gave hope that there might be a way forward. Perhaps it would not be as horrific as she feared.

'At that initial stage I could not have gone to the Internet and printed off useful material but friends did that for me. It was so helpful to read what people around the world were doing about autism and realise that there were ways to give your child the best possible chance within the limitations of his disability. I also received press clippings from all over the world, offering a variety of solutions. I read about swimming with dolphins in California, different diets, various injections. David and I had a laugh over some of the more ridiculous suggestions. We could have spent a fortune on alternative therapies if we had gone along with them all but at least it began to give us hope that out of it all there might be something we could do to help Peter.'

The opinion of the paediatrician did not count definitively with the local health board – it was merely the first step in diagnosis. Peter had to see a variety of professionals, including a psychiatrist and a social worker, and undergo a wide range of tests. The requirement was to have five different opinions in agreement before he could get on to the waiting list for any of the health professionals such as a speech therapist or occupational therapist who might help him practically. Rosie was totally frustrated by all the waiting for these endless appointments.

One morning she found herself yet again in a waiting room with Peter. His behaviour was dreadful and Rosie was conscious of the silent disapproval of those around her. She became very angry at having to go through the public humiliation, particularly as a teacher, of being unable to control her own son. Forty minutes in a waiting room with an autistic child is a very long time. When she eventually gained access to the person they had to see, Peter could not tolerate having the necessary headphones on his ears for the hearing test. As she sat and cried uncontrollably, Rosie was stunned to hear the comment, 'Have you not got over this yet?' It was six weeks since she had received the diagnosis. She could not believe that the supposed professional was showing such a lack of understanding of the nightmare she was living through, particularly after witnessing her traumatic experience in the waiting room.

'If it happened now, I would write and point out that this was not a helpful comment, but at that stage I was feeling very vulnerable and very scared. I just felt hurt and misunderstood.' She could not understand why someone had not thought that the first appointment in the morning might be better for an autistic child, rather than expecting him to sit for a prolonged period of time in a waiting room.

Peter's behaviour was getting worse, with tantrums becoming longer and more intense each day. As he lay kicking and screaming on the floor, David and Rosie would look helplessly at each other and wonder, terrified, what lay ahead. Is this what their life was going to be like? They could visualise the years stretching out before them, with Peter getting older and increasingly difficult to deal with. In public Rosie coped with these episodes as calmly as she could, but returned home physically exhausted and emotionally drained.

Despite the trauma of their own suffering, Rosie and David tried to protect six-year-old Ellen by keeping her life as normal as possible. She picked up information about Peter at her own pace, gradually coming to understand all that made him different from other children. When she asked why Peter was seeing the speech therapist, Rosie told her, 'He can't talk so he has to learn how to do it.' As she realised that Peter had to see other professionals also, she began to build up a rounded picture of his situation.

They received the diagnosis in March 2003. Hannah, a 20-year-old Careforce volunteer, had been working with the church young people during the year, and as they became busy with summer exams she had some extra time at her disposal. Concerned about Peter and interested in the whole field of autism, she did some research, went to Scotland to do a training course and came back full of enthusiasm and new ideas on how to help him. She decided to defer her October entry to Queen's University in Belfast and instead spend the year working with him full time.

This was a godsend for Rosie. Hannah had a very creative mind and though fond of Peter, was less emotionally involved than his mother. Rather than crying about the problem, she was constantly thinking ahead about how to deal with it. She was also very determined – she tried a new idea every day until she found a solution. Gratefully, Rosie acknowledged that Hannah had been sent to them for a purpose.

'When I first heard about Peter I thought, *I can't cope. I'm confused. I need help and it's all so expensive. What route do we take?* One theory contradicted another and I was scared of getting it wrong.'

Hannah in contrast was decisive. 'Peter's behaviour is the biggest problem so let's deal with that first.' Full of youthful energy, bright and keen to develop new skills, she relished the challenge. Hannah's enthusiastic support helped Rosie not just to survive but to look ahead with some kind of hope for the future.

In January 2004 David was due to go on sabbatical for several months to Vancouver, where he planned to study at Regent College. Peter's diagnosis now raised uncertainty as to whether or not the family should go. He was on various waiting lists for help in Ireland and if they left the country he would miss his place and go to the end of every list. Plans for Vancouver, however, were all in place and, as Rosie and David talked about it, they felt David needed the break. They decided to go ahead. Because Hannah was going to spend the year helping Peter, she would go along too as part of the family.

It was at this stage that Anne, a work colleague, came to Rosie one day with a telephone number.

'Why don't you contact my friend Siobhan in Belfast?' she suggested. 'She has been working with her little boy who has autism and he has done very well.'

Rosie had received many such suggestions before. Usually she pinned them on a board on her kitchen wall and did nothing further. Somehow she could never bring herself to follow up these possibilities that might offer hope but would probably only lead to disappointment in the end.

For some reason, however, she decided to act on this one. She telephoned Siobhan and was encouraged by her story. Siobhan had been following a behavioural intervention programme with her son, supervised once a month by a consultant who flew across from London to give help and advice. This consultant had recently moved to Vancouver and now flew to the UK once a year from there. Rosie was sufficiently intrigued by Siobhan's story to contact Bohdanna Popowycz Kram in Vancouver and was very impressed. She seemed to know a great deal about the whole subject of autism and had had very good results in the past. Rosie explained that they were planning to come to Vancouver for several months.

'My books are full at the moment but we will work out something for you when you are here,' promised Bohdanna.

Suddenly this was one of the most exciting things Rosie had heard in her life. This world-famous consultant was going to be in Vancouver to advise them. All at once there was hope. As Rosie read the stories of those who had used the programme, she became more and more enthused with the idea of being able to intervene in Peter's situation and help him develop to his full potential. She could not wait to get to Vancouver and meet Bohdanna in person.

In preparation for starting the early intervention programme with Peter, Rosie was advised to play with him in a structured way for a couple of sessions each day, trying to get his attention and maintain eye contact, while at the same time working on his (as yet non-verbal) communication skills. For two months Rosie and Hannah persevered doggedly with this, finding it difficult to see any progress. One day, however, their spirits were lifted by a surprise telephone call from Siobhan in Belfast.

'Bohdanna is coming to visit in November. Would you like me to bring her down to Enniskillen to meet you and Peter?'

Would they? Rosie and Hannah could hardly believe it was happening. The only suitable time was first thing on Sunday morning, so they skipped church and waited with bated breath for Bohdanna's arrival. Like a whirlwind, Bohdanna descended on the house, exchanged the customary greetings and immediately embarked on a three-hour introductory workshop, showing them how to get Peter's attention and help him learn.

Bohdanna had a 'goody bag' full of all sorts of wonderful things, but one in particular proved fascinating for Peter – a little spinning top with flashing lights. She managed to persuade Peter to do all sorts of things for her in exchange for a few seconds playing with the top, and each time she gave it she modelled the word 'Top' several times before handing it over. It wasn't long till Peter was shouting 'Top! Top!' in order to get his reward more quickly. Rosie and Hannah looked on in disbelief. For months they had tried to get Peter to learn a new word and here was a complete stranger achieving it in minutes. The experience gave them real hope that Peter could learn to talk, if only they could motivate him the way Bohdanna's top did! They had never learned so much about autism, or indeed about anything, in so short a time. Their heads were spinning almost as much as the top by the time Bohdanna left but her visit was a turning point in Rosie's autism journey, giving her the firm belief that Peter could learn to talk after all.

In January 2004 the family, accompanied by Hannah, arrived on the campus of the University of British Columbia, where they would live for the next seven months. Soon after their arrival, they had a visit from one of the staff at Bohdanna's clinic, Sean Bozosi, who explained exactly how to get a programme running, including how to recruit and train therapists. Rosie and Hannah had great fun putting up posters around the campus (with a very cute photo of Peter) and had their first response within minutes. Interviewing and selecting from among so many talented and enthusiastic young people wasn't easy, but very quickly they gathered a great team of four therapists together and soon had Peter's programme running for six hours each day, from Monday to Friday. It was good for Peter to relate to as wide a variety of people as possible and the students soon became very attached to him. The family's experience in Vancouver became dominated by Peter's programme.

Once a week, they had a visit from Sean and at the end of each month they made the hour-long journey to Bohdanna's clinic, by bus and skytrain, so that she could review Peter's progress personally. The first session was disappointing, when Peter refused to co-operate in these alien surroundings. By the second visit, however, Rosie was delighted to see him carry out many of the tasks asked of him. These visits to the clinic were always encouraging, filled with laughter as well as learning, and Rosie was pleased to watch Peter progress from month to month.

Despite the hope now offered by the programme, however, and the concentration that it required, these months on the whole were a dark time for Rosie, especially over the first anniversary of the initial diagnosis in March and the visit to the paediatrician two weeks later. She relived all the happenings of the year before and grieved more fully the loss of Peter as she had believed him to be. David, immersed in sabbatical studies, seemed very content in the library of Regent College. Rosie felt her path of grief was longer and deeper, very different from that of her husband.

She did, however, want to give this programme her very best effort. Of the many different early intervention programmes available, this one focused on modifying the undesirable aspects of the child's behaviour, with a strong social element teaching Peter how to relate to others. The time recommended was thirty-five hours per week. Rosie committed herself to working with Peter every day from Monday to Saturday for the foreseeable future. The daily schedule was split into two-hourly sessions: 9–11 a.m., 12–2 p.m. and 3–5 p.m., stopping for food and exercise in between. For the next two years Rosie followed this very intensive regime with little deviation.

Peter's behaviour was a constant challenge. At one stage he was having one tantrum after another. Because he had very limited vocabulary and did not know how to communicate what he wanted, he showed his frustration by thumping, kicking and working himself into a state. Rosie did not want that to continue as he grew older and knew that in order to modify this behaviour she would have to be ruthless.

One of the hallmarks of autism is rigidity of behaviour – the child feels there is only one way to do something and causes a great commotion if it is done differently. One parent Rosie knew found she could only park in one particular place in the supermarket car park – if she tried to park anywhere else her autistic son would have a tantrum. Parents find themselves trapped in these rigid situations and try to fit into them for the sake of peace. Rosie found that if Peter always wanted to turn right and she decided to turn left, he would either throw himself on the pavement kicking and screaming or try to run away altogether. She knew that the only way to break this behaviour was to persist in going left. To do so was very traumatic for Peter at first, but each time was better, as he gradually learned that he did not have to go by a predictable route. A few weeks later, they were able to go out for a walk and go in any direction without trouble. The training process, however, was very demanding on

Rosie, a vast drain on her emotional resources. She understood why parents often gave up and capitulated to the child's demands.

At one stage when she went grocery shopping with Peter, there was only one set route round the supermarket that he would accept. Any variation produced a tantrum. Rosie and Hannah decided this was something they needed to work on and so nine o'clock every morning found them in the supermarket with Peter. Day after day they took him round the shop in every direction, over and over again, until he could go anywhere and accept that he did not have to go in just one direction. The intervention programme gave them the necessary support while they worked on this aspect of Peter's behaviour.

This particular system worked on the premise that as soon as rigid behaviour appeared, it was important to deal with it immediately, because it would be easier today than tomorrow. Now, six years on, Peter still forms rigid behaviours, but he knows they will get broken the next day. He quickly realises that no behaviour pattern will be allowed to become set.

At the time of his diagnosis, Peter's brain was like a blank page. He did not understand that every object had a name, such as a cup or a spoon. To help him learn, Rosie would touch the cup and then with Peter's hand on the cup she would repeat the name. When they switched to a different cup, his brain did not generalise, so he did not realise that the slightly different object was also a cup. It took many repetitions to learn this lesson. They then moved on to the same process with the spoon, prompting him to learn the name. Gradually, painfully slowly, he learned the names of the common objects in his world.

The next challenge was to teach Peter how to communicate what he wanted. To do this, Rosie used the Picture Exchange Communication System (PECS). A board was put up in the kitchen with pictures of a number of items that Peter might want. When he brought Rosie the relevant picture, it elicited a response, so he learned that when he brought her the picture of a biscuit, he received an actual biscuit in exchange. They were working on the whole concept of communication, because Peter did not understand that he could get something by asking for it in words – he thought the only way he could solve a problem was by screaming. The picture board worked well and he quickly got the idea. Even if he brought the picture ten times, he found that it worked! Each time he brought the picture, Rosie matched it with a word.

'Biscuit. Yes, you can have one.'

Once Peter realised that the word was linked to the picture and began to say it, the picture was removed from the board so that he could only get what he wanted by using the relevant word. Gradually he learned he had to use a phrase to achieve the response, 'I want biscuit,' and eventually a full sentence, 'I want a biscuit, please, Mummy.' Success!

Peter had no innate problem-solving abilities whatsoever and had to be taught things that other children worked out automatically. Although toilet training is always a big challenge for children with autism, Peter was toilet trained by the age of 3, which was a great achievement for him. The first time he found the toilet lid down, however, he sat on top of it – he did not have the ability to work out that he had to lift the lid. That next step always had to be taught to him. One day he was intrigued with magnetic darts that stuck to the dartboard when thrown. When a couple of the darts stuck to each other he was baffled, not realising he could pull them apart. Once he was shown what to do, he would remember what he was taught if he was sufficiently motivated, but mundane daily tasks presented much more of a difficulty. These had to be shown over and over again before he remembered.

This detailed teaching took great patience and Rosie often became frustrated with his slow progress. She was aware that it required a very large investment for a very small return. She grieved for the loss of her own teaching career, which she loved but which had to be sacrificed to Peter's programme. The programme was also expensive and she was very grateful for a small inheritance they received at that time, which helped them pay for it, and later to the local Education and Library Board who provided generous funding for two years. 'To be able to afford to have someone like Bohdanna walk into your home and help once a week was invaluable. Without that expert advice, working out how to solve a child's individual problems would be impossible in the time frame.'

As the family's return to Ireland approached, Rosie found herself in something of a dilemma. She had found it inspiring to live on the university campus, receiving so much help from the students. She did not think that the family could manage to follow the programme in the same way back in Enniskillen, without their help. One solution was to find an apartment in Belfast near Queen's University so that Rosie could live there with Peter during the week, from Monday to Friday, with local students to help in his programme.

As they thought through the implications of this plan, Rosie was very aware of the drawbacks, but felt they had to trust God with the outcome. 'Lord, stop us if this is completely mad,' she prayed. As they proceeded, everything seemed to fall into place and they felt clearly that God was leading and providing as they found a suitable apartment and prepared for Rosie and Peter to move in. As they began to let people know their plans, however, they were dismayed at the response.

'It's not fair on Ellen. She's going to feel abandoned by her mother from Monday to Friday while Peter gets all the attention.'

'It's not going to make any difference to Peter. Nothing can really be done to help him. There's no point breaking up the family like that.'

Rosie felt she had to fight through the discouragements.

'It has been the area of my life where I have felt most mis-understood. I think people felt I was clutching at straws. I know you can't cure autism – but I wanted to give not only Peter, but also Ellen, David and myself the best life possible. When we decided to proceed with this plan, people thought we had taken leave of our senses. Looking back now it was probably not necessary to go to those lengths, but I would not have missed that year in Belfast. I really learned how to run the programme because I had no other focus there and did vir-tually nothing else.' Hannah, now a student at Queen's University, was still available to help with Peter and to train other students to work with him. From time to time Hannah would babysit while Rosie did other things to bring some sense of balance to her life. It was a bizarre situation but Peter's programme ran very well.

Despite the dark warnings from some that they would never recover normal relationships again as a family, they received huge support from the church congregation in Enniskillen. Some of the ladies did wonderful activities with Ellen to compensate for not having her mother around during the week, reading books, knitting dolls' clothes, baking cakes. Rosie made sure that she and Ellen kept in touch through long phone calls and on Saturdays they went out and had special mother and daughter time together.

As the Cupples family were flying to Vancouver in January 2004, two ladies from the autism clinic in Vancouver had been on their way to Belfast to set up a similar one there. Returning from Vancouver in September, Peter was able to slot straight into the Belfast programme which was by then fully opera-tional. The regular input in Vancouver had been very helpful in terms of getting him started and Rosie was glad to be able to continue with weekly supervisory visits in Belfast. By the time Rosie and Peter returned to live in Enniskillen at the end of that school year, Peter was ready to start going to nursery school, so fortnightly visits were sufficient. As people had predicted, it was difficult for the family to readjust to living together again in Enniskillen but they worked through it. On balance, Rosie felt that, though strange, that year had been very worthwhile.

Back in Enniskillen, Rosie realised again the lack of provision for autism in the local area. With Peter reaching the age for school, they decided to let him try mainstream education, and chose a little rural school with a strong provision for special needs. One of the ladies helping with Peter's home programme successfully applied for the job as his classroom assistant, to great rejoicing in the Cupples household. He was going to school with someone who knew him very well and knew how to work with him, giving continuity between home and school, which was very important to Peter. Rosie knew that when he went to school he would be able to sit at his desk and follow instructions without upsetting the classroom routine. A teacher herself, she did not want to impose a disruptive child on the teacher. The teacher's comment was, 'He's the most obedient child in the class.' Rosie understood what she meant because as a result of his programme Peter now obeyed instructions automatically.

Five years later, Peter is still in mainstream education. However, the school situation has to be regularly reviewed, as each year the gap between Peter and other children widens. Rosie is aware that he will not be able to continue there indefinitely. At the age of 9 he fits in well to the classroom routine and the other children try to include him in everything – even when he does not want to be included! The work done with Peter at school is meaningful and realistic and he benefits from all the fun of school, including going on school trips. He enters into what is happening in any way he can, playing his part in school assemblies and concerts.

Rosie chuckles, 'He has his costume and gets dressed up just like other children. When he takes the microphone and says his lines, other parents are as pleased to see Peter taking part as they are to watch their own children.' Thankful that school has worked out as well as it possibly could do for Peter, Rosie is conscious that his attainments are far from those of other children of his age.

She knows that for now teaching staff are happy for him to be in mainstream school, but one day they will tell her that they feel Peter has reached his limit. Provision exists in special schools for autistic children with the most severe needs and major behavioural problems, but there is little provision in the educational system for children whose parents have worked with them intensively at home. 'In an ideal world it would be lovely to have a school for autistic children whose parents had worked with them, where the children could continue to be stimulated and developed. At the moment the choice is between putting him into a school where he is miles ahead of others or a school like the one he is in, where he is miles behind them.'

Autism is often not diagnosed until children are older. This may be due to a number of factors, but sometimes it is because parents find it difficult to cope with the school investigating. Facing the problem and telling people about it has helped Rosie deal with the situation but she recognises that not everyone reacts in that way. To her, being able to use the early intervention programme has meant doing something positive to help Peter.

She knows from experience that anyone undertaking such a programme can easily find themselves plagued with irrational guilt when doing ordinary chores such as shopping or ironing – anything not directly connected with their child's development. It is hard to escape from the idea that every day counts – every day of uncorrected behaviour makes it much more difficult to correct later. Rosie felt every minute of every day needed to be spent with Peter because tomorrow might be too late.

One piece of advice from Siobhan, the Belfast mother whose son had done so well in the programme, always resounded in Rosie's head: 'You have a window of opportunity in Peter's early years and you can't afford to miss it.'

Rosie comments, 'Although the principle is correct, it enslaved me. I gave up life for those years. Yet I couldn't take the risk of not doing it. I needed to be able to go to bed at night feeling that I had done my best for my child that day. Through all the madness of the year in Belfast I kept thinking, *At least I have done my best.*'

Rosie is deeply appreciative of the devotion and commitment of those who have given up their time to help with Peter's programme. 'One of the most enriching experiences of our lives has been getting to know these helpers. This amazing group of young people were in our house for hours each week and we have come to know them really well. We still have three who come to help with Peter after school. Perhaps the best thing to come out of this whole situation has been the great worldwide network of people that we would not have met otherwise.'

These days Rosie can count on Peter to behave almost anywhere. Recently she filled in a questionnaire which asked, 'Before you did the programme could you take your child to . . .' and there was a list of all the places where they might take Peter. When it came to the section on 'After the programme . . .' she was able to tick all the boxes except the theatre. 'We haven't managed to get him to sit quietly yet. We will get there because it's just a matter of training him and building it up gradually from a short time to longer. We just haven't got there yet.' Because Rosie taught Peter to be flexible as a small child, both he and the family now benefit. He can accept the change in routine that allows them to go on holiday, for example, something which many families with an autistic child find very difficult.

While grateful for all the progress Peter has made, Rosie is realistic about the situation. 'Peter has achieved a great deal for a child with autism, but he is very different from a child who doesn't have autism. He's also progressed significantly compared to autistic children who have not been involved in a programme like this. Autism continues to be the great unknown. Peter is growing and developing and sometimes it can be in all sorts of new, unpleasant and undesirable directions. Each day a new challenging behaviour can appear. We try to keep a step ahead but it is a work in progress. We continue to work very hard on behaviour and social interaction. In some ways we are delighted with his progress: he has good eye contact and good relationships within the family. He will give me a hug and a great welcome back when I return after being out, but outside his family and helpers he has much less awareness of others, especially children, which is very disappointing for us.'

Another frustration is that although Peter can now talk and has the language to communicate most things, he has little motivation to do so. He has learned to use speech in order to express his wants but, at the age of 9, he is still largely limited to functional speech. When he does make comments they reflect the concrete nature of his thinking: 'Daddy has a blue jumper.' 'Mum is sitting on a chair.' 'Ellen is playing the piano.' The family are delighted to hear Peter talking, but would love him to be able to communicate with them more fully.

Having learned how to obtain what he wants, however, he has also moved on to learn that he does not always get an immediate response – sometimes he has to wait. He understands 'Not now, but after dinner,' or 'We'll go there later – another day.' He can accept postponement as long as he knows it will happen sometime. If he is told something will happen 'very soon' he cannot tell what length of time that might be. He needs to know in concrete terms what is going to happen. To help his concept of time he has a picture board about today, yesterday and tomorrow. The picture board works because he can grasp what happened yesterday and today. Tomorrow is much more difficult for him to understand.

When Rosie began the programme, one of the questions she asked was, 'What is a realistic goal for us to have for Peter?'

She was told, 'By the age of 7 he should be able to tell you what he has done at school.'

At the time that seemed an impossible dream to Rosie, yet now he is indeed able to respond to that question – albeit on his own terms. One day, just before he was 7, Rosie picked him up from school and asked, 'Well, what did you do at school today?'

'I ate an apple and a banana. I had chips.'

He could tell her all he had eaten at school that day because he is highly motivated by food. When Rosie asked about the other children at school there was little response, but he did tell her that he had played on the computer. She realised how well he could communicate about things that were important to him. It was far from communication as it is generally understood, but for Peter it was a big achievement towards which he had worked really hard. Everything with autism is to do with motivation and because Peter is motivated differently from other children it affects how he communicates. Rosie comments, 'Some days he is not motivated – like us all he has good days and bad days but on the whole life now is much easier than it is for many families living with autism.'

With the wisdom of hindsight, Rosie realises that her early optimism was excessive. 'The people who write books are those with great results, with children who get a good outcome. Not everyone who uses the programme has the outcome they hope for. But you need to read those stories about the parents whose children are now coping in a mainstream school without a classroom assistant, relating positively to other children, in order to know what is possible and give yourself hope.'

It is still a challenge finding meaningful things for Peter to do and integrating everyone's needs into the family. He enjoys being outdoors and going for long walks, while Ellen is not so enthusiastic about all this walking. She is interested in history and enjoys visiting National Trust properties, which is not always the easiest outing with Peter. Rosie says ruefully, 'He tends to be noisy during the tour but on the whole people are understanding. Sometimes if we're in a group of people I tell them at the outset that Peter is autistic, before something happens. Some people I know carry little cards which they give out, explaining the situation. I have never felt the need to do that but everyone copes in a different way.'

For Ellen, now approaching her teenage years, it has been a very interesting journey and having Hannah as an extra person in the family has been a hugely enriching situation for her. At school she once wrote, 'I live with my mother, my father, a sort of sister and a brother who has autism.' In Rosie's eyes the greatest proof of how well Ellen has handled the whole situation is the fact that she has never said anything negative about Peter.

'I know relationships may change as the children grow older and Ellen becomes more independent but up to the present she has coped supremely well. At the end of the day Peter is her little brother and she looks out for him. She is as excited as anyone else at his progress.' Ellen understands that he has a disability, but is very matter of fact about his condition, introducing him casually to her friends, 'This is my brother Peter and he has a brain problem.' She doesn't want them to be expecting too much from him.

Rosie's greatest fear was that Peter's autism would be a blight on Ellen's life but, on the contrary, it has proved to be a valuable experience for her, helping her become a very caring person. 'She gives and gives without expecting anything in return,' says Rosie. 'Some days she is keen to interact with him and he looks through her and walks away. Other days he shows his excitement when she appears. When she returned after being away for a week at drama school, at first Peter appeared unconcerned, but ten minutes later he suddenly became excited at the fact she was there. It seemed to take a while for the penny to drop.'

The family try to include Peter to the maximum in their life together. He always says grace before they eat. He is learning to empty the dishwasher so that he can make his contribution. When Rosie originally began the intervention programme, her hope was that one day he could live independently. That dream does not look promising at the moment, but she is determined to be optimistic.

'Rob Parsons of Care for the Family often says, "Don't read the score at half-time." I have never doubted that Peter is the child God gave us. God has a reason for placing Peter in our family and teaching us many of the lessons we need to learn through him. He has a purpose for Peter. The promise we originally claimed for him was, "On this rock I will build my church" (Matt. 16:18) and we had hopes that he would one day play a significant role in bringing God's kingdom here on Earth. I still believe that God can build his church through Peter as well as through others. He is part of God's plan and God will be in charge of where his life goes.'

Rosie's faith was not always so strong. At one training day she attended, another Christian mother said to her, 'I know my little boy's future is in God's hands.' Struggling to come to terms with Peter's diagnosis, Rosie's immediate response was, 'That's not where I'm at.' Seven years on, she is coming closer to that position now. She is learning not to worry so much about Peter. She has a friend at church who lives with very challenging circumstances and one day she confided in him regarding her worries about the future.

'Shut the door – don't go that way,' was his advice. 'Live life today.'

Rosie decided his words were wise. 'That is one of the big things I have learned through Peter's autism. I have learned to live one day at a time, to shut the door on scary thoughts and not let my imagination run away with me. I concentrate on appreciating the good things about today and the fact that we now have a relatively normal family life and do things that other families do most of the time.'

Rosie is aware of how fortunate she is in many ways. While some parents of autistic children have to attend church on alternate weeks, taking turns to mind their child at home, she has never had to miss church because of Peter – he has gradually learned to sit through the service. He loves the echo in the church, so he tends to make sounds so that he can hear the echo, but his minister father can cope with that. Out of deference to a visiting speaker, Rosie tends to put him in the crèche where he is happy to sit and play with toys. She is glad that this is the case, because finding babysitters can be a challenge – people may be willing, but they feel intimidated by the situation. When the children were younger, babysitters tended to entertain Ellen while she looked after Peter. Now that Ellen is getting older and going out more often in the evenings, babysitters are needed who can look after Peter on his own. Fortunately the girls who help with him during the day are usually available in the evening also, but Rosie is aware that she is very dependent on them. 'If we ever moved house, the first goal would be to recruit a large babysitting team and get them all round to bond with Peter.'

Looking at the positives in her situation, Rosie is conscious that she had a very special provision in Hannah, who shared the load in the early years. Being both mother and teacher is a difficult combination for any mother, even if autism is not part of the equation. Rosie appreciates the huge role filled by Hannah. She says, 'I have learned about one to one teaching with Peter and can do it, but Hannah was a natural. Whatever she does, she does 100 per cent. She was on the Internet doing research, sifting through information, focusing on what was important. I have been so fortunate to have her. I recognise that no one else has a Hannah.'

Overwhelmed by the situation, many mothers with autistic children end up suffering from depression. Often the marriage cannot take the strain of the disability, resulting in a single-parenting situation, which makes it even more difficult. Peter sleeps all night, unlike most autistic children whose disrupted sleep patterns are a severe strain on parents. He likes tidiness and hates mess – one of the advantages of this being that he was out of nappies overnight by the time he was 3 years old.

Rosie still finds some aspects of Peter's behaviour very disturbing but she tries to remind herself that it is usually a transitory phase. At one stage he was obsessed with spinning round and round, which she found very annoying. Other strange behaviours occur that are inappropriate, but she holds on to the knowledge that in time they too will pass. Sending out prayer requests to an extensive email list, she appreciates the genuine support received from all their friends. 'It has been hugely encouraging to meet people who have obviously read the emails and know in detail what Peter's needs are. On days when I felt alone it was a real encouragement to know that a great group of people were praying. Friends often felt helpless, but this was one very valuable thing they could do to support us.'

Despite all Rosie's positive thinking, however, the feeling of loss is still very real. As Ellen approaches her teenage years, Rosie revels in the fact that she and Ellen can go out for coffee and go shopping together. At the same time, she is always conscious that David will never have this kind of relationship with Peter. When she struggles with the situation, she is thrown back on the question that came to her when she first received the diagnosis: 'How do you cope without strong foundations in your relationship with God?'

On the first Sunday of 2003, just a couple of months before Peter's diagnosis, Rosie was gripped by the words of a Bible verse projected onto the screen in church before the service began: 'Unless a grain of wheat falls into the earth and dies it remains alone, but if it dies, it bears much fruit' (John 12:24, ESV). Unsure why it seemed so significant, she nonetheless felt God was highlighting it for her in a special way. 'At that point I knew nothing of the dying process I would go through in our situation with Peter – the dying of my own hopes, dreams, desires. "If it dies it bears much fruit." I have no idea what the verse will fully mean for me as things develop in the future, but I will find out. All I know is that God, who has been with me this far, goes with me into what lies ahead. I trust him for the fruit.'

So do not fear, for I am with you; do not be dismayed, for I am your God. I will strengthen you and help you; I will uphold you with my righteous right hand.
Isaiah 41:10

3

Joyful in Hope

Casually, Karen ran the vacuum cleaner over the living room floor. Another few days and she would be returning to the exciting buzz of university life in Belfast. Suddenly the door opened and her father and sisters appeared. Her father's face was grim and an apprehension that was almost physical gripped Karen's stomach as he hesitated in the doorway.

She bent over to switch off the vacuum cleaner. 'How is she?'

His eyes filled with tears. Dismayed, she looked at Rhonda and Sandra. They appeared stunned.

'What is it?' she asked, her voice shrill with fear.

'It's cancer.'

Karen sat down. Silently the others came and sat near her. Rhonda perched on the arm of the sofa, and put an arm round Karen's shoulders.

'She's been ill all summer. Why has it taken until now to find the problem?' protested Karen.

'I don't know.' Her father sighed heavily. 'The doctors say she has oesophageal cancer which has spread to her stomach and there is nothing they can do at this stage.'

'Nothing they can do?' Karen could not take it in. This couldn't be happening.

It was her first contact with cancer. It seemed too brutal that her mother, the pivotal figure in the family, should be taken from them like this. It was 16 September 1986.

About to start her final year at university, Karen struggled to come to terms with the news.

Why us? Why is my 12-year-old brother going to be left without a mother? My Dad is only 46, why should he be left without his wife at this age? Why does it have to strike our family? Karen was plagued with questions – she questioned herself, questioned the doctors, questioned God.

A few weeks later, Karen went into her mother's bedroom as usual to say goodnight before she returned to university. Her mother had been unable to speak for the last three weeks, a traumatic experience for all of them. In some ways Karen felt she had a lighter sentence than the others, shielded, at university, from her mother's daily suffering but seeing a clear deterioration every weekend as she returned home. That Sunday night Karen kissed her goodbye and left. The next day, she was at university as usual when her mother passed away peacefully in her sleep, less than five weeks after diagnosis.

In the wake of their mother's death, Karen and her two sisters were very conscious of the spectre of cancer hanging over the family. Since it had taken her mother at such a young age, the likelihood of one of them also getting cancer in their forties was high. Given the current statistic that one in three will be affected by cancer at some stage in life, they wondered which one of the three sisters it would be.

In 2005, Karen celebrated her fortieth birthday. In April of the following year, she was at work when her phone rang and the receptionist informed her that Sandra, her younger sister, had called in to see her. Something serious must have happened if that was the case, because her family lived in a different part of the country and rarely came to her workplace. Suddenly she remembered that Sandra had been to see a consultant in Belfast City Hospital that morning, and a feeling of dread came over her as she walked down to reception.

Showing Sandra and her husband into an empty office, Karen turned to face her. 'I'm the one who has it,' Sandra said simply.

Karen was stunned. Although they had talked together about the possibility of one of them having cancer, the actuality was a shock. Automatically she said, 'Sandra, can I pray for you?' The sisters had never before openly discussed their faith or their relationship with God. Now Sandra and her husband, Gary, sat with bowed heads as Karen prayed a very simple but intense prayer.

'God, if it is your will, please make Sandra better.' It was one of the most moving moments of Karen's life.

Throughout her mother's illness and death, Karen had had the invincible conviction of youth that she could survive without support. Twenty years on, she was very aware of her need for God and his strength to help her deal with the situation. A few weeks after Sandra was diagnosed, Karen went with her to a service at her church. Deeply moved, they stood with arms round each other, tears running down their faces, as they sang the song 'My Jesus My Saviour'. They knew that Jesus was their only real 'comfort' and 'shelter' as they faced the future.

From May to November, Sandra had surgery followed by chemotherapy and radiotherapy. At the end of that time, tests showed she was completely clear of cancer. She was feeling well and relieved that it was all over.

Shortly after Sandra's diagnosis, Karen's father made a suggestion. 'Karen, why don't you get checked out?'

She raised her eyebrows in surprise. 'Why should I get checked? If it hits one in three, there is no chance of anyone else in the family getting it.'

'No,' said her father gently, 'it doesn't work like that. My doctor's advice is that all of you should have a medical check-up.'

Unconcerned, but happy to put her father's mind at rest, Karen and Rhonda arranged to go for tests.

Through the charity Action Cancer, they had initial mammograms and a few weeks later both received letters referring them to the City Hospital for further investigation. Rhonda was concerned, as she had discovered a breast lump. Karen was in Euro Disney with her daughter when she received a text: 'I've got the all clear! It was just a cyst; they've drained it and I'm fine.' Karen thought, *Great! One out of two. By next week it'll be one out of three.*

The following Monday, Sandra arrived at Karen's house to go to the hospital with her. She had been through her first chemo session two weeks earlier and her beautiful long dark hair had started to fall out. She arrived wearing her wig and looked fantastic. The two sisters headed off to the City Hospital as if they were going for a day out, having a laugh together in the car on the way there.

The consultant was pleasant but thorough. 'I can't feel any lumps but we'll do another mammogram and, if necessary, we'll do an ultrasound and perhaps a needle biopsy.' Three and a half hours later, Karen and Sandra were sitting outside the doctor's office. One by one, other patients went in to see the doctor and emerged a short time later smiling in relief, until at last only Sandra and Karen were left in the waiting area.

Turning to Sandra, Karen said, 'I've got it too.'

'What do you mean?'

'Just look, everyone went in to see the doctor and came out looking happy. No nurse went in with them. Glenda has just gone in now with the doctor.'

Glenda was a nurse who had helped during Sandra's treatment. As Karen and Sandra walked into the office Karen said to Glenda, 'You don't need to tell me. I have it too, don't I?'

'Yes,' said Glenda. 'I'm sorry.'

Although Karen had guessed the result, she was still stunned by the news. They had all been fixated on the idea of 'one in three' and never really thought that more than one of the sisters could have it. Sandra and Karen sat side by side in the doctor's office and cried as they held each other. That both of them should have breast cancer was too much to take in.

The doctor was unable to say when Karen would have surgery or what treatment she could expect. A backlog of patients had built up and there were many unanswered questions about the whole way forward. The one reassuring element for Karen was to look at Sandra and think, *She has been through this and has started her treatment. She has survived this far. I can do it too.* Rather than feeling fear, she was aware of all the people who would be there to support her – hospital, family, friends, neighbours, church.

'I knew that with God's help and the support of all these people, I could get through whatever was to come.'

She received her initial diagnosis on 3 July 2006.

Two days later the consultant telephoned: 'I can fit you in on Saturday for surgery.'

'No,' said Karen, 'I can't go.'

'Why not?'

'I've booked a caravan holiday for the family starting on Saturday and if I told my two children it was cancelled because I was going into hospital they would be heartbroken. Could we postpone it to the following Saturday?'

The consultant agreed and the holiday went ahead.

At the caravan park, Karen and Sandra had caravans side by side. On the first night of the holiday, the sisters went together with some friends to a prayer and healing service in a nearby town. Karen was not sure exactly what she was going to, but found the evening, led by Sharyn and William McKay, deeply uplifting. Healed from terminal cancer in 2004, Sharyn and her husband William now devoted their time to praying for those with cancer. Karen listened spellbound as Sharyn shared her story. It was a new experience to be in a gathering like this, with such a consciousness of faith around her. At the end Sandra and Karen went to the front individually for prayer. As three people laid hands on her and prayed, Karen was aware of a warmth spreading through her body. She did not expect instant healing but knew that she needed God in her situation. She placed her future in God's hands and trusted him with the outcome; she felt an inner strength to face whatever lay ahead.

Karen found it hard to analyse just how prayer helped. She could identify with C.S. Lewis in the film *Shadowlands*, when he said, 'Prayer doesn't change God, it changes me.'[2] During that stressful period before surgery, she felt God reaching out to her in a special way as she put her trust in him. Her prayer was, 'God, if it is your will, make me well.' She knew that God was able to heal miraculously or through medicine, but she also felt that no matter what happened, cancer was not the worst thing in the world. The knowledge of God's presence with her superseded everything.

On the following Saturday, Karen went into hospital for surgery as arranged. She had a partial mastectomy and the removal of lymph nodes in the surrounding area. A few weeks later when she got her results, the type and grade of her cancer turned out to be identical to Sandra's. Described as 'Grade 3 triple-negative', it would not respond to some of the usual drugs.

Looking back, Karen analyses her feelings: 'When you hear you have cancer, the first thought is, "Am I going to die?" Once you realise that death is not imminent, the second question is, "What treatment am I going to have? How is it going to affect me? What side effects will it have?"' For Karen, surgery was to be followed by chemotherapy.

She had six sessions in total. Once every three weeks, a mixture of drugs was fed into her bloodstream intravenously. On 29 August, she realised she was beginning to lose her hair, so when 2-year-old Kate-Lynn had gone to bed, older sister Sophie, to her great delight, was allowed to cut her mother's hair short and then shave her head. It was a great adventure for a 7-year-old. Karen's brother normally kept his head shaved in any case, so when he, Sandra and Karen were together they looked like triplets. Although, for Karen, losing her hair was one of the lowest points of the whole experience, they tried to lighten it by referring to themselves as 'The Baldies'. At the same time, she had always worn her hair long, so to look in the mirror and see herself with none at all was a shock.

As the treatment continued, Karen was overcome by an unfamiliar feeling of lethargy. Her mouth was dry, food had no taste and sleep was difficult. By the fifth chemotherapy session she was feeling pretty grim, the impact of the chemicals on her body growing stronger as the treatment progressed.

Two years before, Karen and her husband Brian had decided that he should give up work and stay at home to look after their two girls full-time. It was a difficult decision to make and Karen, in particular, did a great deal of praying and heart-searching about whether it was the right decision. Now, in the light of her illness, the advantage of that arrangement became clear. Karen could come home after her treatment, Brian collected the girls from school and nursery and looked after them as usual, so to a large extent normal life continued for them. The only difference was that they had their mother at home as well as their father, which was a bonus as far as they were concerned.

Karen and Brian talked to the children about the situation, explaining about their mother's cancer. Because they had already seen Sandra go through her treatment and lose her hair, they accepted hair loss as part of the situation. To 2-year-old Kate-Lynn, it meant simply that mummy was in hospital, mummy had a scar and mummy was at home from work for a while. For Sophie, the greatest thrill was being allowed to act as hairdresser.

As a rule, Brian did not show his emotions or talk about his feelings. He reacted by making the most tempting meals for

Karen, keeping everything together for the home and family, and making sure Karen had time and space when she needed it. He was a solid strength and support, helping to carry her through the whole experience.

Karen drew strength from a number of sources. When Sandra was diagnosed and they prayed together that day, it was a turning point for both of them, allowing them a new openness to talk about their faith. With Sandra's cancer having led to Karen's check-up, she was grateful to Sandra for both her early diagnosis and a positive role-model as she went through her treatment.

Karen's friends in church rallied round to write letters, send texts and pass on books. William and Sharyn McKay's book *Voice of Hope*[3] was particularly inspirational. Psalm 91 became an anchor – during the sleepless nights of her treatment Karen read it every night. Another precious passage was Psalm 34:4: 'I sought the LORD, and he answered me; he delivered me from all my fears.' As she held on to God, Karen was amazed at the number of verses in the Bible that referred to fear and protection. She was very aware of God's arms around her, giving her the strength she needed.

She appreciated the services of the Macmillan Support and Information Centre at the hospital. Counselling and a range of complementary therapies were offered and Karen availed of them all. Each time she had a radiotherapy appointment, she booked a complementary therapy at the same time. Through this she made many friends – amazing people from many different backgrounds, all brought together by their common experience of cancer.

The Ulster Cancer Foundation also provided many services and Karen and Sandra appreciated the help they found in the local support groups. At one of the first groups they attended, a lady stood up and said, 'I am Rosemary and I was diagnosed with breast cancer eighteen years ago. It was the best thing that ever happened to me.' Later, with her treatment behind her, Karen felt she could identify with that sentiment. Since her diagnosis, many things had changed in her life; it had affected her whole attitude. 'I live life now,' she told her friends.

Karen finished her treatment in February 2007. She had a good summer, happy to put the whole experience behind her. In October, however, she found a small lump near the site of her surgery the year before. At her regular check-up with the oncologist she was reassured when he said it was just breast bone and nothing to worry about. However, over the following months she was conscious that it was getting bigger and one night showed it to Sandra who advised her to get it checked again. Next morning Karen rang the surgeon who had done the original operation and made an appointment for the following day. Reassuring her, he sent her for an X-ray. As she sat waiting to see the doctor again after the X-ray, the consultant radiographer came in and said he would like to do a CT scan. Warning bells rang immediately in Karen's mind.

Having private health insurance through the firm she worked for, Karen was able to have the scan carried out that same night. On the screen she saw a nodule on her lung – the radiographer told her it could be one of a number of things and not to worry about it. He said he would send the results back to the surgeon. At ten o'clock the following night the surgeon called to assure her that the nodule on her lung was not related to her original breast cancer. However he would need another CT scan and a PET scan to give a more detailed diagnosis.

She had the PET scan on 10 April, the day after her forty-third birthday. On the evening of 16 April she went to see the oncologist on her own, thinking there was nothing to worry about. As she sat outside his room, waiting to see him, the pathologist went in and stayed for ten minutes. It was not a good sign. As the consultant showed her into his office, he looked solemn. The scan had shown two 'hot spots' – one in the lung and one on the breast bone. He wanted to do an ultrasound and needle biopsy on the chest lump that evening.

As she prepared for the biopsy, Karen clung desperately to the nurse's hand – she needed comfort, not just during the procedure but to face the possible outcome. As she waited for the results she telephoned a nurse friend who happened to be on duty in the clinic that evening; quickly she came to be with her. At nine o'clock the consultant informed her that both lumps were cancerous – a spread from the original breast cancer. He added, 'I know you came to me in October with this. I'm sure you're very disappointed.'

Karen was too shocked to respond. She had been under the impression that the first bout of chemotherapy would have killed any rogue cancer cells and protected her from further cancer in the immediate future. It was a surprise firstly to hear that this was not necessarily the case and secondly that the cancer had spread even though her lymph glands had been clear after the original diagnosis. It took time for her to absorb the news.

The oncologist suggested surgery to remove the lump on the chest wall, followed by chemotherapy for the lung tumour. The surgery turned out to be fairly minor, with no complications, requiring only one day in hospital. Karen recovered quickly and one week after surgery went with Sophie on a One-to-One Challenge weekend run by the charity Care for the Family, where they shared special time together as mother and daughter. Karen determined to make the most of it and entered in to everything, from football to zip wire, with infectious enthusiasm.

Three weeks later, she started chemotherapy for the second time. As before, she would have six sessions, at three-weekly intervals. This time the side effects were more severe. Her nails dried up and began to fall off. Her fingers and toes felt numb and tingling and the skin peeled off her hands and feet. A sensation of total exhaustion left her unable to do anything but lie in bed with the duvet over her head for two weeks following each treatment. She was not physically sick but felt totally taken over by an indescribable fatigue and accompanying depression. Sophie took great delight in being allowed to shave her mother's head again but Karen found the hair loss more difficult the second time. First time round, she and Sandra had done everything together. This time she was alone.

She hated the wig this time. It may have been because it was summer and the wig seemed too hot and itchy. She found scarves cooler and lighter on her head. She also discovered they could be a great fashion accessory; a friend brought her a whole selection of colourful scarves from China so she was able to match them with what she was wearing. She was unable to wear her contact lenses as the chemo made her eyes water constantly but she eventually solved that problem with laser treatment, allowing her to dispense with lenses and glasses altogether.

In mid-July, halfway through the treatment, a scan showed a 25 per cent reduction in the size of the tumour, which was great news and an encouragement to keep going. After the fifth session, however, Karen felt very poorly and at her next appointment the doctor's verdict was, 'I think you've had enough.' In the effervescence of relief, Karen flung her arms round the surprised doctor and kissed him. She was aware of the possible disadvantages of not completing the course but valued her quality of life. At the end of September, she had another scan which, unbelievably, showed no further change in the size of the tumour. She had expected some improvement – she had gone though the second part of the treatment for nothing! According to the doctors, chemotherapy had been her only hope. She was devastated.

Just after the recurrence was diagnosed in April, Karen had heard about the Oasis of Hope hospital in Mexico. In May she and Sandra met with a small group of ladies who had been there and had found the treatment very helpful. The most exciting case was Gillian who, like Karen, had had secondaries from breast cancer in her lungs but now had no detectable lesions.

Having heard their stories, Karen decided she would go to Mexico. Conventional medicine seemed to offer her little, apart from chemotherapy. Oasis of Hope, on the other hand, offered a combination of conventional and alternative therapies, nutrition, exercise, counselling, education, prayer and uplifting activities. The holistic approach appealed to Karen and seemed to make sense. It was certainly worth a try.

The next question was funding. The whole expedition was going to be formidably expensive. As family and friends heard about it, however, offers of help began to come in. One friend paid for the flights. Sandra held a stew and quiz night. Karen's father donated the cheque he received for summer work on his brother-in-law's farm. Groups of friends organised sponsored walks and coffee mornings. Fundraising events in her workplace raised £12,000. Friends at church had a fundraising dinner and one friend raised money through the Christmas lights display at her house.

Although Karen had not lived in Warrenpoint for twenty-five years, the local community there adopted her cause. On the Old Warrenpoint Forum website[4] neighbours and childhood friends posted messages of encouragement and support and the website appeal brought in donations from all over the world. People were generous, kind and thoughtful. Karen was buoyed up by all this warmth and goodwill. Cards, letters and little notes flooded in, even from those she did not know personally. She could not believe the response. At some fundraising events, Karen did not know half the people who were there but they had heard her story and come along to support her. Within six weeks she had all the money needed for the trip. The generosity of people in the midst of a global credit crunch was overwhelming.

Making the decision to go to Mexico and getting involved in the preparations gave her a positive focus. When the medical paperwork for Mexico came through from the Belfast hospital, she was taken aback to discover that not only had the tumour not improved after chemotherapy, it had actually increased in size. Karen was stunned. 'At first it was like another kick in the teeth. However, I knew the treatment in Mexico was going to work anyway, regardless of the size of the tumour, so I got over it quickly.' She was looking forward to the trip, although naturally concerned about leaving Brian and the children for eighteen days. As she and Sandra flew out from Dublin, prayers were going up from people of many church backgrounds, as friends united in their support.

Tired and somewhat apprehensive, Karen and Sandra arrived in Tijuana late on the evening of 16 November and went straight to the Oasis of Hope hospital. They were shown into a beautiful, spacious room where they gratefully fell into bed and woke the next morning to a glorious sunrise. Determined not to miss anything, they got up in time for the 8 a.m. service. After a time of praise, accompanied by guitar, everyone in turn shared things for which they were thankful – a very positive start to the day. Psalm 91 was the reading that first morning and the service was followed by hugs all round. Karen found herself hugging people she had never met before, but happily accepted hugging as part of the atmosphere of the hospital.

Bruce and Vicky, the American couple who led the service, were working in the hospital as full-time missionaries. Shortly after being diagnosed with cancer in 1997, Bruce had a dream in which he was taking painless medication on a beach. When he came to Oasis of Hope for treatment, the dream actually came true as in those days patients could take their IV drip to the beach. Together with friends who had accompanied them to Mexico, they set up a ministry visiting and praying with the patients. Ten years later, Bruce and Vicky decided to give up their jobs and work full time as 'amigos de esperanza' – 'friends of hope' in the hospital.

Although the whole ethos and approach was based on a living faith and trust in God, not everyone attending the hospital was a Christian. For those who wished to draw on their faith in God as part of their healing process, however, opportunities were constantly available. On Monday evening, a prayer and share time helped new folk settle in at the beginning of the week. Friendships were quickly formed as people bonded with others in similar circumstances, experiencing the same questions and fears. Bruce and Vicky visited each room daily and prayed with people individually if they wished. On Tuesday evening there was a prayer and healing service. After dinner on Thursday evening, a fun sing-along gave everyone the opportunity to take part, participating on percussion instruments of every description. The songs ranged from amusing ones about hospital situations, sung to tunes everyone knew, to Christian songs allowing people once again to affirm their faith. At the Sunday morning service, they had the opportunity to hear Dr Francisco Contreras, the Director of the hospital, preach the sermon.

Karen discovered that Oasis of Hope, founded by Dr Contreras's father in 1963, had treated more than a hundred thousand patients from fifty-five countries. Using a multidisciplinary approach to meet the physical, emotional and spiritual needs of its patients, the emphasis was on living with cancer as positively as possible. Patients were encouraged to control cancer as they would an illness such as diabetes, through diet, medication and a variety of alternative therapies. Tijuana, where the hospital was situated, was a city with many problems but the hospital area with its easy access to the beach stood like a real oasis within its own environment.

Ozone therapy was Karen's first treatment each day. Ozone is a high concentration of oxygen (O_3 rather than O_2) that is thought to inhibit cancer in the body. Each morning, Thomas, the nurse, took her blood and in a pouch added ozone, until it went bright pink in colour. On the first morning, as Thomas shook up her blood before putting it back in her body, he danced around in time to the gospel music playing in the background. Although the whole situation seemed surreal, Karen appreciated the humour and laughed with him. A variety of intravenous treatments followed, including vitamins C, K and B_{17}. Sometimes she was on the IV drip for eight hours at a time. She was also on oxygen and swallowed a total of forty-three tablets per day, supplements to protect her body and raise her immunity.

Sandra and Karen both appreciated the helpful talks about nutrition and living with cancer. The relaxation sessions and lectures about mind and body were useful for Karen in the ongoing situation and for Sandra as she considered future prevention. The sisters, already close, enjoyed the peace and rest of the hospital atmosphere together. They also made many friends from different parts of the world. Karen realised that many people there were in a worse situation than she was and became quite emotionally involved, in particular with some of the younger patients. At the same time it was encouraging to see some transformed in the short time between arriving and leaving.

For Karen and Sandra the eighteen days were quite intense, and some days treatment lasted most of the day, but Karen found it all very peaceful. The doctors were very approachable and had time to sit on the bed and talk. The atmosphere was warm and welcoming, the staff and volunteers loving and caring. Karen comments, 'Most hospitals I do not want to go into – this was very different; it was all such a positive experience.'

The time seemed to pass rapidly and soon they were saying goodbye to the friends they had bonded with so quickly. People would return to the hospital at different times depending on where they lived in the world, so Karen would not necessarily meet the same people again. She left with suitcases packed with enough medication to cover a three-month home care programme of injections and pills until she returned in February.

On her return to Ireland, Karen was aware that something had changed in her. 'I feel so different now. I don't feel I have a death sentence hanging over me, which I did before. I'm more positive about life and, though I don't plan too far ahead, I'm not worried about the future. Matthew 6:34 tells us to take each day as it comes and not to worry about tomorrow. I used to plan ahead and think "What if . . ." I don't do that anymore because it does not add one day to my life. That is the big change for me.'

At the same time, Karen was conscious that January 2009 would bring a visit to the oncologist in Belfast and another scan, with all the questions that would raise. She did not want any more chemotherapy, preferring the Oasis of Hope home regime of forty-three pills each day and three injections per week. At least she now felt more in control of her future. She had prayed intensely about whether to go to Mexico or not and saw her answer when so many people pulled together and provided the resources for her to go. Now it was all over to God. She was trusting that his wish for her was long life, whether with cancer or without, but she was willing to accept his will, whatever that turned out to be. Six months earlier, her only focus had been getting rid of the cancer – now she had handed over all her worries about it completely to him. She felt a sense of release and peace; it was a lovely feeling.

Karen arrived back from Mexico on 4 December 2008, Sophie's tenth birthday. Her birthday party was held two days later, which a slightly jet-lagged Karen was delighted to be able to host. With Brian at home, as usual, with the children, Karen knew that their routine had not been disrupted to any great extent when she went to Mexico. Sophie had shouldered responsibility and tried to help Brian as much as possible while Karen was away. In Mexico the thought had even crossed Karen's mind, 'They could cope without me if anything did happen to me.' When she arrived home, however, she realised how untrue that was. The children were overjoyed to see her and in the weeks following her return, showered her with hugs and kisses. Kate-Lynn, soon to be 5, wanted reassurance that her mother was not going away again, which was difficult for Karen to deal with. As they thought ahead to the return visit to Mexico in February, Karen and Brian decided that for the sake of the girls he should again remain at home and her older sister Rhonda would accompany her.

Karen gratefully spent Christmas quietly at home with Brian, the girls and her father. Boxing Day was always the biggest day of the holiday, when the family gathered at her father's house in Warrenpoint. All the cousins were delighted to meet up in an excited crowd of children and presents. Karen looked around the seventeen members of her family, appreciating them in a new way. As usual, her father did the cooking – the menu supplemented with a variety of contributions from the day before. In the hallway all the children sat at a long trestle table covered with a Christmas tablecloth, while the adults had a more decorous meal in the dining room. Afterwards the youngest child gave out the presents and encouraged everyone to guess the contents. That night they stayed overnight with Karen's dad, always a treat for the children.

All over Christmas, however, at the back of Karen's mind, was the consciousness that her next scan was coming up on 6

January. She hoped it would be good news. Kate-Lynn's fifth birthday was the following Saturday and she wanted to be able to celebrate with her. With some trepidation she made her way to the hospital on Tuesday, and waited nervously until Thursday for the results. Her hopes for a good report were dashed. The tumour on her right lung had grown by 50 per cent. Karen was upset and depressed. How could it have grown so quickly? What did she do now?

Faced with the facts, the oncologist came to a decision. 'Let's leave it for eight weeks and if it hasn't changed by the end of that time then we might consider surgery.'

Surgery! This was the first time since the secondary diagnosis that surgery had been mentioned as an option. The oncologist explained that surgery is often not an option for secondaries if there are a number of lesions but in Karen's case the single large tumour on her right lung might well be operable.

One week later Karen obtained a copy of the report and, as she read it, she realised that she also had a spot on her left lung which the doctor had not mentioned. When she asked him about it, he dismissed it as being so minor as to be insignificant. Karen knew she had a choice to make. 'If he's not worrying about it, then I'm not going to worry about it,' she decided. That night she emailed her doctor in Mexico to give her the results and ask for a telephone consultation. A couple of days later the doctor called. Karen was concerned and disheartened that her trip to Mexico had had no effect on the cancer, but the doctor was reassuring.

'Look, Karen, it's only been six weeks since you started treatment here. It won't work overnight. Keep on with the diet and persevere.' It was encouraging to get a second opinion and hear that the doctor did not think all was lost.

Karen began to put in place plans for Rhonda and herself to go back to Mexico for the follow-up week in February. In order to cut down costs she arranged to get a PICC line – a thin flexible tube inserted into one of the large veins in the arm to make it easier to have blood tests and treatment – put into her arm in Belfast before she went. Despite everyone's best efforts, however, Karen's veins refused to take the PICC line. The only option was a return to hospital later in the week to have a central line put into one of the large veins in her chest, just under her collar bone. With the flight to Mexico booked for Saturday, Karen had her case packed before she went to hospital on Friday.

It turned out to be a very stressful nine hours. Once her blood tests were taken in the morning she spent all day waiting without food or drink in case she needed a general anaesthetic. From time to time someone would ask, 'Are you staying overnight tonight?' to which she kept replying, 'No, I'm flying to Mexico in the morning!' Eventually, late in the afternoon, she was taken to theatre where the central line was successfully inserted with the aid of a local anaesthetic.

'How can you do this so close to my date for flying?' Karen asked the doctor.

'Only if I puncture your lung will you not be flying,' he replied. 'But the chances of that are very remote!'

Thankfully the procedure was carried out without any problems, and eventually Karen managed to escape after 7 p.m. She drove home, had dinner, finished packing, called in at church to say goodbye to Sophie at youth club and drove to Warrenpoint to stay overnight with Rhonda before their early flight the next day. It had been an exhausting process but worth it all when she reached Mexico and the line worked beautifully.

Arriving in Mexico for the second time was totally different. Knowing what was at the end of the long journey made travelling less stressful and the familiar faces of the hospital staff were reassuring. Disappointingly, there was no overlap with patients from her previous visit, but she enjoyed making new friends. The treatments she received were the same as in November so there was no fear factor. Vicky and Bruce, who had been such a help before, were still there, accompanied this time by two volunteers.

As she discussed her scan and the option of surgery, the doctors in Mexico were reassuring and agreed with the Belfast oncologist that surgery was the right way to go. The wide choice of healthy fresh fruit, vegetables and juices was wonderful, fully appreciated by Karen now that she knew all the work involved in preparing them at home. Rhonda also enjoyed the food but organised an occasional escape to the neighbouring Starbucks to satisfy her coffee addiction.

During the week, Karen again enjoyed the talks dealing with the effect of the mind on cancer, but the greatest benefit from the week was spiritual. Times of prayer each morning started the day on the right note and healing services brought a sense of calm to mind and body in the evening. There seemed to be a special mix of people in Oasis of Hope that week and, in the peaceful atmosphere, confidences were shared and friendships formed. Once more the comradeship of having cancer surmounted all other barriers. People of all ages and all geographical and religious backgrounds had come together with a common purpose. As Karen listened to their stories she felt humbled by their strong faith that God could intervene in their situation.

She realised that almost no one had fear in their eyes. Moved by the power of the Holy Spirit in the meetings, they cried and laughed as they prayed together and shared their deepest feelings. Faith was strong and spirits high, despite the circumstances. Rhonda, who had some reservations about the spiritual side, enjoyed the fun element, especially the Thursday after-dinner sing-along. As they left at the end of the week, Karen felt a renewed sense of optimism about the future.

'No one knows how long their life is going to be. I have seen the Mexico experience add months or years to the life of others. It has been very worthwhile, however long it adds to my life. I'm looking forward with confidence and hope.'

Back in Ireland, a scan showed that the tumour in her right lung was stable so surgery was still an option. Video-aided technology meant that two small apertures would allow an implement to cut and stitch all in one action and remove the tumour without being overly invasive. Her hope was that it would all be over within a few weeks so that she could get back to work after Easter. The best news was that she would have no further chemotherapy at present.

She continued to find support and help from a variety of sources. Each Monday evening and Friday lunchtime, she attended a healing service in St Anne's Cathedral in Belfast. She met regularly with a small group from the prayer ministry team in her church for prayer and her home group was a constant support both spiritually and practically. During the school holidays, friends from the group looked after the children when needed. Others turned up at the door with home-cooked meals. Men from the group got to know Brian – playing golf, befriending him and taking him away from the situation from time to time. The group prayed constantly, with her and for her. All of this helped to strengthen her faith and contribute to a sense of well-being and the knowledge that God was with her.

Before Karen's surgery, she and Brian decided to take the family to England on holiday, as she would be in hospital over the Easter break. They had a very exciting visit to Alton Towers theme park and then on to Cadbury World in Birmingham, where the girls were mesmerised by the process of chocolate making and thrilled with the plentiful free samples.

In early April, back in Belfast, keyhole surgery to remove the 2½ cm tumour from Karen's right lung went ahead as planned. She expected to make a quick recovery but was shocked to find it was a number of weeks before she felt anywhere near normal. She had extensive bruising over her body, which amused her.

'I was black and blue for a month and a half. It was so bad I thought they had dropped me off the table! The consultant said I had lost so much blood during surgery that it caused widespread bruising.'

At the end of May, scan results were disconcerting. Although the tumour had been removed from her right lung, another one of similar size had now appeared there. Tumours in the other lung had also grown significantly. More chemotherapy was the only option to stop the progress of the cancer. Despite all her positive thinking, Karen was depressed once more. She had so hoped for a better result and was experiencing no obvious symptoms. Instead of going back to work on 9 June as planned, she went to break the news that she was facing more chemotherapy and an indefinite postponement of her return.

The oncologist was keen to start treatment immediately, but Karen took time to weigh up her options. Once she started chemotherapy, she knew she would probably be feeling unwell for some time. There were things she really wanted to do. The family were due to go on holiday to Portugal in a few weeks' time so, with the oncologist's agreement, she decided to postpone treatment until after their return. When she told the girls she was going to have chemotherapy again, Sophie was somewhat concerned that with Karen not returning to work, she would be at home to keep a close eye on her homework and after-school activities.

Despite the prospect of the holiday, Karen found it difficult not to be depressed as she thought about the progression of the cancer and the necessary treatment ahead. Then she realised that she had a seven-week chemotherapy-free window which she could enjoy with the family rather than waste in pointless despondency. In the weeks before treatment began, she did all she could to boost her body's natural defences. She took regular exercise, walking with a friend. She kept to the Oasis of Hope diet, which she sometimes found restrictive and difficult, but realised it was worthwhile. 'When I am tempted to eat the wrong things I think, "A slice of chocolate cake, or another month with my family? No contest!"'

She also decided to have oxygen therapy in an attempt to boost her immune system. Hyperbaric oxygen therapy (HBOT) is the medical use of oxygen at a level higher than atmospheric pressure. It is thought that treatment in a hyperbaric chamber, which floods the body with pure oxygen, can promote healing and cell regeneration. She had this treatment five days a week in the weeks leading up to chemotherapy.

At the beginning of June she was pleased to be invited to share her experiences with a Belfast group of the Ulster Cancer Foundation. The audience was inspired by her energetic approach and positive attitude. The following week she spoke at a fundraising dinner held by the Lisburn Soroptimists Society, where £7,000 was raised for cancer charities.

She aimed to pack as much as possible in to the weeks before chemotherapy started. She had always wanted to climb Slieve Donard, the highest peak in Northern Ireland, on the edge of the Mourne Mountains. On 20 June, friends received a triumphant text, 'Having lunch at the top of Slieve Donard!'

Although the Portugal holiday was already arranged, Karen realised they had a few free weeks before that. They had planned to take the girls to Disney World in Florida the following year, but given the present situation they decided not to put it off. An Internet search threw up a good deal and they had eleven glorious days in Florida, returned home to three days of feverish laundry, and set off again for the planned fortnight in Portugal. She wanted to store up as many happy memories as possible for Sophie and Kate-Lynn. By this stage the girls were accepting multiple holidays as normal.

Both holidays were very useful in taking Karen's mind off what lay ahead. She had priceless time with the girls and Brian, and it was refreshing to interact for a short time with strangers who did not know her story and treated her like everyone else. For the duration of the time away she was largely able to shut the door on cancer and isolate it in another room in her mind. Her attitude was, 'I can't stress about it every day. I'm just going to have this month without stress and worry. I'm making a conscious decision to live and enjoy the experiences of today.' She read, chilled out, explored and played with the family. As it all came to an end, however, Karen knew she had to come home to the hard reality of thinking again about chemotherapy and cancer.

She held the verse from 1 John 4:18 constantly in her mind: 'Where God's love is, there is no fear, because God's perfect love drives out fear' (NCV). Although she had no fear for herself, as she looked ahead Karen's concern was constantly for Sophie and Kate-Lynn. More than anything else, she wanted them to grow up with a strong faith in God and committed to him. Godparents were not a tradition in her church, but she wanted the girls to have positive, spiritual role models and mentors, whatever lay ahead. When she approached her friends Hilary and David about taking on the role of godparents, they were honoured to be asked and very willing to accept.

On their return from holiday, Brian's brother Gary came from England for a fifteen-day visit, with his 16-year-old daughter and 10-year-old son. Karen took the lead in organising the activities and together the two families toured Northern Ireland, reminiscing with Gary, who had been out of the country for twenty-five years. Because of the visitors, they did things together that they might not have otherwise done with the girls. This extended family time was very special, and when chemotherapy started in the middle of the visit, Karen determinedly kept it in perspective and carried on entertaining the guests.

During this time the family also acquired a dog. The girls had always looked after their grandmother's dog when she was away from home, but they really wanted one of their own. Karen postponed the idea, thinking about the work it would entail, but while they were in Portugal Sophie kept raising the subject. 'When are we going to get a dog? Can we have one when we go back home?' Karen was non-committal, but a few days after their return Rhonda telephoned her.

'You know how you've been talking about getting a dog for the girls? I know someone who is looking for a home for a miniature Schnauzer. Why don't we go and have a look?'

That weekend, while members of the extended family were all together at a family birthday party, Karen and Rhonda went to see the dog. They immediately fell in love with Tilly and took her with them there and then, back to the party. Letting Tilly out of the car, they walked nonchalantly round to the back of the house, where the children were all playing outside. The girls' faces were a picture.

'Look at the dog! Who owns it?'

'Would you like it to be ours?' Karen was casual.

Shrieks of delight greeted this proposal and Tilly became part of the family. Kate-Lynn enjoyed dressing her up like a baby doll, Sophie posed with her, but Karen, as she had anticipated, ended up looking after her.

In September, Sophie and Kate-Lynn started attending a course one evening per week called CLIMB – Children's Lives Include Moments of Bravery. This six-week course, run by the Ulster Cancer Foundation, was for children who had a significant adult with cancer. The aim was to try to explain to children between the ages of 5 and 12 the relevant facts about cancer and its treatment and answer questions that children might not ask at home. For an hour and a half each week they had the opportunity to talk about their feelings and how they dealt with them. Separate groups for older and younger children encouraged them to talk in a way appropriate to their understanding. Sophie's height meant that most people treated her as older than her 10 years, but this course gave her the opportunity to be a child with her own feelings, rather than being seen in her usual role as older sister.

Karen hoped that the course would enable the children to talk to her more freely about their feelings. While they were there, she spent the time making memory books for them. In words, photographs and scanned images, she recorded the details of their birth, their reactions as young children, their baby identity bracelets, hospital cards and stories about their funny little ways as toddlers. Photographs prompted bittersweet memories as Karen relived the wonder of their early years as a young family.

Once the children's memory books were completed, Karen's aim was to do one for each of her sisters. She was consciously ticking things off a list of things to do. 'If I had fifty years to live I would still do things as I am doing them now,' she said. 'The principles of living are still the same. It's all about living in the present but preparing for the future.' In September she read a book entitled *One Month to Live*.[5] She read it slowly, thinking about the questions at the end of each chapter and recording her answers. 'This book asks the question – if there was no tomorrow, how would you do things differently today? Asking such questions helps anyone put their life in order.'

Chemotherapy this time was in the form of pills, avoiding the trauma of finding veins. Karen simply added more pills to those she was already taking each day. Once again, she was facing six three-week cycles and by the second cycle she was tiring easily and aware that she was more on edge than usual.

'What if this treatment doesn't work?' she asked the oncologist.

'Well, there's not much more we can give you. We're running out of ideas.'

'Is there any research I could get involved in?' She was willing to try anything.

The oncologist was not hopeful. 'There are some trials going on at the City Hospital but I'm afraid they are not a suitable option for you.'

It was discouraging news, leaving Karen struggling to cope with the implications. In August the consultant had said to her, 'Do let us know if you have any symptoms you are concerned about.' Those words made it difficult not to think that every twinge was linked to the progression of cancer. In September she was conscious of a nagging pain in her right side, and a troublesome cough had developed over recent weeks. Keeping her imagination in check was becoming increasingly difficult.

Scans at the end of September revealed that the chemotherapy had been unsuccessful. In addition to the existing tumours, a new one had appeared on the back of her skull. For this she would have five sessions of radiotherapy, which would reduce it and ease the headaches, but leave her with a bald patch at the back of her head. Once the radiotherapy was completed, they would try a new chemotherapy drug.

In addition, Karen felt she had to explore any other avenue that might be helpful. She started attending Synergy Healthcare, a centre in Belfast offering complementary therapies such as ozone haemotherapy and intravenous vitamin C. She did not know if they would work, but she wanted to try anything that might slow down the progression of the disease.

'If they're running out of choices, what can I do? I can't get my head around giving up. I'm doing as much as possible to find something that helps, but also keep myself busy so that I don't dwell on things. I like to feel I am doing something for someone else rather than focusing totally on my own situation.'

She continued with her work with the Ulster Cancer Foundation. She began helping with a weekly coffee morning for army wives whose husbands were in Afghanistan. She joined a dance class and took the dog to obedience classes. Life was full and interesting.

She was determined to enjoy life, and planned a number of trips away. The family enjoyed a lovely time together in Longleat, England, over the October half-term holiday. However, they returned home to the news that a good friend had died suddenly from a heart attack at the age of 61. Karen contrasted this sudden death with her own situation. 'I realised that with my illness I had been given a chance to appreciate all that I have and to prepare my family for a time when I would not be with them. God's blessings are shown in many different ways.'

When the scan results in September were not good, she had decided to book herself and her two sisters, Rhonda and Sandra, on a Mediterranean cruise. They laughed their way round Europe, calling in to Cannes, Genoa, Florence, Pisa, Rome and Naples. They enjoyed relaxing together, reminiscing over recent years and appreciating all that they meant to each other. Karen savoured the opportunity to spend time with her sisters after more than twenty years of living separate lives. Again she saw it as a positive of her illness – this was something she would not have done if she had not had cancer.

In November she started the new course of chemotherapy. Apart from feeling sick for the first few days after each treatment, life continued with some normality. She began to prepare for Christmas and look forward to spending time with the extended family. The thought was never far from her mind that this was probably her last Christmas Day, Boxing Day and New Year's Eve with the ones she loved. She refused to be sad, however, and the family concentrated on making it a very joyous and special time. Karen found words in Romans 12:12 which became meaningful to her and helped her through the whole holiday period: 'Be joyful in hope, patient in affliction, faithful in prayer.' She tried to live it out each day.

In January she went on a five-day holiday to Tenerife with her father, a special time just for the two of them. They had not spent that amount of time together since she left home to go to university when she was eighteen. With no other members of the family around, and conscious of the time pressure of her illness, she felt as if she was getting to know him again in a new way.

On return from holiday, further tests assessed how well the latest chemotherapy drug was working. Karen was shocked to discover that, far from it being successful, tumours had now appeared in her liver, spine and pelvis. An MRI scan showed two brain tumours. She was devastated. Why had God not answered her prayers? So many people were praying for her healing but God had still not intervened. An unforeseen outcome of the brain tumours was even more disturbing – she was no longer allowed to drive. Her independence had been taken away.

A few hours after receiving this news, Karen was sitting in the weekly Monday evening service in St Anne's cathedral. That evening, Bishop Harold Millar spoke of how life's restrictions can turn into something positive. Karen immediately began to think of all the friends she could call on in the coming days, weeks and months to help her out – getting to radiotherapy and chemotherapy sessions, picking up the girls, taking her on outings. She says, 'Suddenly a wonderful thought came to me – I would never go anywhere alone again. This was God's way of letting me know he was still with me.'

In February she had radiotherapy for the brain tumours, every day for a week, followed by more chemotherapy. She describes the month, however, as one of 'celebration and thanks'. She invested in a new wig, which made her look and feel great, her work colleagues organised an evening out for her, and her sister held a Table Quiz Charity night to raise money for some of the charities which had been of help to her. 'It was a night to meet my friends and relations and to show them that no matter how bad the news, I was still fighting and I still had God by my side.' Her daughter Sophie did very well in her entrance tests for secondary school and Karen now had a new focus: 'My dream is to see her in her new school uniform at the beginning of September.'

At the same time, she was human and she could not always be positive. Around this time she confessed, 'Night is the hardest time, when the fears came flooding in. That's when I plan my funeral. There are some songs that are particularly meaningful to me that I would like to have.' As she faced her fears, she found the counselling service provided by the Ulster Cancer Foundation a source of great support. She was realistic about the future if the miracle did not happen and began helping Brian to plan ahead, looking at the children's needs and milestones over the course of a year – birthdays, new school uniform, Christmas – and lining up support for him from friends and family.

Karen does not know what the future holds but she believes that God has a purpose for what he allows into our lives. 'This cancer has helped me understand that ultimately we are not in control. God controls our lives and so we don't have to fear the future. And also that life is not all about me. When you've been through an experience like this, you realise that the world is vast; as an individual I'm only a little part of it. God's purposes are wide and all-embracing. I was very career-oriented before. This has helped me realise that getting to the top of the ladder is not the greatest thing in life. Love and friendship and family are all important. Knowing God's forgiveness for the past and strength for the future is vital. Faith in God is our ultimate security.

'My plans for the coming months are to enjoy life but to keep praying for healing, for peace of mind and not to feel too ill if the illness progresses further. I thank God for each new day and for the friends and family that have loved and supported me.'

Be joyful in hope, patient in affliction, faithful in prayer.
Romans 12:12

Postscript

Karen passed away on 4 May 2010, just two weeks after hosting a coffee morning at her home, which raised £2,500 for a local cancer charity.

4

Not Second Best

'Where do you think we should go on holiday this year? What do you think about Thailand?'

'I'm not sure. It'll be hard to improve on South America. I've always quite fancied going to China.'

Henry and Mary pored over the brochures. Where to go on holiday was one of their major annual decisions. With fulfilling jobs, a comfortable home and plentiful leisure time, life was good. At some appropriate stage in the future they would have children, but there were many other things to do first.

They had been married for around five years when it began to occur to Mary that having children might not be an automatic next step. Looking back, she can't believe how naive they were. 'You don't think about time running out. A lot of people put off having children because of their career but that wasn't the case for us; we just wanted to enjoy the things we could do together – weekends away, unusual holiday destinations. We were oblivious to the fact that the opportunity to have children wouldn't last forever. We thought that whenever we decided we wanted to start a family, it would just work out. We were taken aback when we did decide that the time was right and then nothing happened.'

They decided to seek medical advice – perhaps some minor problem preventing Mary becoming pregnant could be easily rectified. The doctor made arrangements for her to have

investigations done in the autumn, after their planned holiday in Thailand. In September, however, Mary realised that
she might be pregnant and, with some excitement, did a test
which to their great delight proved positive. When her doctor
confirmed that this was indeed the case, they gratefully cancelled the planned hospital investigation and excitedly began
planning for a new baby. All went well until the end of
October when, without warning, Mary had a miscarriage and
suddenly their world seemed to implode.

Up to that point, Mary and Henry felt they had experienced
a full range of emotions – the desire to have a child, the longing for something to happen, the recurring disappointment,
the euphoria when Mary became pregnant. When they lost the
baby, however, they experienced a grief and depression they
had never known before. With her emotional and mental situation no doubt complicated by hormonal changes, Mary felt
totally bereft.

Unable to talk about it to others, Mary and Henry soldiered
through the experience with little external support. With the
exception of a few members of the family and one or two close
friends, no one was aware of what had happened. Mary's
teacher colleagues knew merely that she was not at work
because she was ill. She refused to discuss the details. Their
friends in church were also oblivious. Mary did not want
people to feel sorry for her; she could not cope with their pity
– although looking back now she realises how much of a mistake that was. 'I didn't want to talk to anyone. More than anything else, I was feeling very angry with God. We had prayed
so much for a child. Why had he let this happen? How could
he claim to be a good God and allow our baby to die – this
baby we had waited so long for?'

While Mary was wrestling with all this, Henry was doing
his best to support her and keep her spirits up, despite his own
pain. The bereavement process, which can drive some couples

apart, actually brought them closer together. Reluctant to talk to anyone else, they talked a great deal about it to each other. For Mary, there were countless triggers that upset her and renewed her grief. She felt unable to escape from a stream of expectant mothers who crossed her path. Henry commented wryly that she could spot a pregnant woman from a mile away.

Seemingly constant birth announcements from friends perpetuated the agony. Happy mothers with their children underlined her childless status, especially new parents bringing their children for baptism in church. Although she did not resent others having children, she found it difficult to be around them. Her emotions were so raw that she was unable to look at new babies or small children without the sight of them stirring up the grief in her heart again. Church became one of the most difficult places to be, with so much activity revolving around families and children.

She became very depressed and at times felt so low that there seemed no point in going on. 'It was like a big black hole that I felt I would never get out of. I was praying about the situation and yet I felt God wasn't showing me the way forward. I felt he had let me down. It wasn't true. I realise looking back that it was a case of seeing his footprints in the sand where he carried me, but I say that now, very much with hindsight. Going through it at the time, it was very different. Rather than my faith carrying me through, I would say that God carried me through. I could not see what he was doing.'

Much later, when people heard about the miscarriage, a well-meaning friend patted her on the arm and said consolingly, 'It just wasn't meant to happen.' Rather than being comforted, Mary was outraged. 'I felt that was one of the worst things to say to someone who had lost a baby, because that's not how I saw it. I thought, *No, losing a child couldn't be meant to happen.*' She was upset by comments from people who thought they were helpfully looking on the bright side: 'Lucky you, you can go off on great holidays. We're staying in Ireland with the kids again.' 'You've no ties; you're free to go out at night whenever you want.'

Her reaction was bitter. 'Those things are really hurtful to people who have no children and wish they had. We would have given it all up to have children. Nothing else mattered in the end.'

Although their pattern had been to talk through everything together, there came a time when Mary felt so low that she even shut Henry out. One half-term was particularly black. 'I would never have done anything to myself because I believe God gives life and is in control of when we live and die, but I did feel life wasn't worth living. Nothing Henry could say helped me. I knew that talking together was vital but I became quite selfish and wrapped up in my own emotions. Henry was going through it too, but as a woman I felt it was my own personal problem. I thought, as a man, he could not have any real understanding of the maternal instincts within me that were being denied.'

Looking back, Henry and Mary regret not being more open about their feelings of grief at the loss of their baby. They realise now the support and strength they could have gained, particularly from those who had been through a similar experience. There was no need for them to feel isolated and alone. As individuals and as a couple they had a need to grieve and to receive support while they adjusted to what was happening in their lives.

Eventually, Mary went in to hospital for the postponed investigations. She underwent a range of tests and treatment, each time with the hope that it would have some effect on the situation. At one stage she had a series of injections to create more eggs. Each time she had more tests and tried some different treatment, it created more stress as they waited in desperate hope for a positive result.

Looking back now, Mary realises they went into IVF rather naively, without really thinking through the different possibilities and their significance from a Christian perspective. They would not have wanted to destroy any fertilised eggs, but at the time, perhaps because Mary was not producing many eggs, the possibility did not even occur to them. She believes that God overruled in the situation, shielding them from having to face that decision.

The indignity and intrusiveness of the treatment was stressful for both of them; it was invasive medically and psychologically. Yet they were willing to go through anything and lose any inhibitions they had, if it meant they could have a child. The injections upset Mary hormonally, leaving her emotionally fragile, but underneath she was buoyed up by the hope that this would work.

'When I got the fertilised egg implanted, I spent two weeks wondering, *Will it take? Will it take?* Inevitably my mind would imagine what it would be like if it happened. How amazing it would be to hold our own child! Then I realised I was not going to get pregnant this time either, and my emotions plummeted again.'

They went through this rollercoaster of emotions three times. Each time it failed, Mary's immediate thought was, *Now we have to start the whole thing over again.* She knew that there was no guarantee and yet she refused to accept that it would not work.

In the middle of all this, Mary's close friend telephoned her. 'I know this is not a good time for you to hear this,' she said, 'but I am pregnant again.' What could Mary say? 'Oh, it's not a problem. That's lovely. I am delighted.'

She was indeed delighted for her friend but inside her heart was crying out, 'Why? It's her third child and I can't even have one.'

The insatiable longing for a child, deep down in the centre of her being, had grown until it obliterated everything else.

Their fulfilling jobs brought them enviable salaries, they could buy what they wanted and go on exciting holidays whenever they wished, but the deepest desire of their hearts was something they could not buy. Mary was aware how fixated she had become.

'I tried to think it out logically and I knew that some people didn't have children. Perhaps the Lord didn't want certain people to have children but I prayed, "Don't let it be me." I felt completely selfish.'

When the third attempt at IVF was unsuccessful, Henry and Mary reluctantly decided it was not going to work and that God was closing that particular door for them. Desperately looking for support, they attended a local group for couples in their situation, interested to hear what others were feeling and how they were dealing with it. Perhaps because it was such a personal thing, they found the group of limited help. Everyone's story was unique and Mary left the group with the longing that she would be different and that it would happen for her.

During the third session of IVF, Henry and Mary were already thinking about adoption. They had done some reading on the subject and talked together about whether it was something they should consider. If it was impossible to have a child any other way, it was certainly another option. Deciding to explore the possibilities, they went ahead and applied to their local health trust. A social worker came to visit them but was unable to take the matter any further while they were still undergoing IVF treatment.

In 1990, the plight of thousands of children in the care of state orphanages in Romania came to the attention of Western media. Graphic stories of the Romanian orphans, many disabled, mentally ill and abandoned, sparked off the possibility of an overseas adoption in Mary's mind. Together, she and Henry talked informally to a number of people involved in the adoption process and to couples who had adopted children from overseas. Suddenly it seemed an exciting idea, and yet, sitting in Northern Ireland, it hardly seemed feasible. From her conversations with the social worker, Mary knew she was too old to be considered for adoption of a baby in Northern Ireland, although there might be a chance of adopting an older child. They decided to pursue the idea of overseas adoption and see where it led.

On completion of the third course of IVF, with no hope of a pregnancy, they began the official adoption process – a series of twelve two-hour sessions with a social worker. The basic procedure would be the same whether the proposed adoption was in Ireland or overseas, although when they eventually decided on an overseas adoption it involved a few extra sessions dealing with specific issues. The first shock, at the initial session, was to discover that the social worker was pregnant.

'She asked me if I minded,' said Mary, 'and of course I said no, but I did find it difficult.' Nonetheless, they knew that this was the path they had to follow, and although they found the process stressful and mentally invasive, they were determined to give it their best efforts. Each week they were given a topic to think about and prepare together before discussing it with the social worker. Subjects ranged from their attitude to finance to whether or not Mary would give up her work, from toilet training to dealing with difficulties that an adopted child might bring.

There was only one meeting which they felt did not go well. It was to do with the subject of discipline, where a casual comment led the conversation on until it acquired greater significance than it deserved. At the following session, Henry and Mary brought up the subject again and talked through the issues more cogently this time. The social worker appreciated their approach and the fact that they had taken time to revisit the topic. Mary looks back on it all now: 'Anyone wishing to adopt needs to realise that it is a long, invasive process, but you can get through it. It's just a matter of taking one session at a time.'

Henry and Mary did not divulge to family or friends that they were going through the adoption assessment, not wanting to have to deal with telling the whole family if they were rejected for adoption. One evening, Mary's brother and his wife called to see them while the social worker was there and were nonplussed at being turned away at the door. At the risk of seeming ungracious, Mary did not want them to know what was going on.

Mary had a secret memory from years before of her mother talking about someone going through the adoption procedure and how the social worker had inspected the bed to see if their sheets were clean. 'It wasn't like that at all,' Mary says now, 'but I always had this niggle at the back of my mind that my housework would be found lacking in some way on the day the social worker called.'

One day, just before one of the social worker's visits, a bomb exploded in the Belfast suburb where Henry and Mary lived, blowing in the French windows leading onto their patio. They had to do that particular interview with the window boarded up. Throughout the evening Mary's thought was, *If we survive this, we'll survive anything.*

As the meetings progressed, Henry and Mary wondered increasingly whether they were coming up to the required standard, as the social worker gave no feedback on how they were doing. At last, at the final meeting, she confirmed that she would be recommending them as adoptive parents. Overjoyed, Henry and Mary confessed to her their fears that they might not have come up to the mark. She seemed surprised.

'Did you not realise that I would not have gone on through twelve sessions if I wasn't going to recommend you?' she asked. Henry and Mary had not worked that out. The main thing was that they had been given the go-ahead for adoption. Because of their age, they only had a year and a half in which they could adopt abroad, so they began to make enquiries immediately.

With Romania featuring so prominently in the news, Henry and Mary wondered if God was pointing them in that direction. Their initial enquiries with local social services had not received a very positive response – demand to adopt children from Romania was high and at that stage they had still been receiving IVF treatment so could not pursue it in any case. They wondered about South America but had heard of children being purchased from there and were very definite that they did not want to go down that road.

They were hoping they could adopt a baby. The more they thought about the whole situation, the more the desire grew within their hearts to help a young child from overseas and give him or her the opportunity of a life that would be impossible otherwise. They realised that there were many couples in Ireland wanting to adopt locally, so a child in Ireland would have a much better chance of being adopted than one overseas. In the end, the actual overseas country they dealt with would be of secondary importance, as long as they could find a child to whom they could offer a loving, positive future.

One Sunday evening, before the adoption process was complete, the speaker at their local church service was a friend Henry knew from work, who had adopted two children from Northern Ireland. After the service, he gave Henry and Mary a telephone number for the Northern Ireland representative of the South American Missionary Society (SAMS) who, in turn, had contacts in Brazil for children needing adoption. Suddenly it seemed as if a door might be opening. Hearing of another family who had adopted two children from Brazil,

Henry and Mary went to visit them. They enjoyed the visit and found it helpful, but the children were aged 9 and 11 and they left thinking that they really wanted to adopt a much younger child. Another couple, who had adopted a baby from Sri Lanka, gave them great encouragement to keep going and pursue their dream.

At the beginning of the summer, Henry and Mary were officially given the go-ahead for an overseas adoption although, in preparation, a large number of documents would have to be notarised. Fortunately, they were introduced to a solicitor involved with the Catholic adoption agency, who was very kind in helping them through this process. Once they got clearance, they excitedly shared their plans with the family, but were unprepared for the mixed reaction they received. While understanding their desire for a child, the family had some concerns about their decision.

'Are you sure you're doing the right thing?'

'Some of these children can be very disturbed.'

'Make sure the child is healthy.'

By this stage, however, Henry and Mary were sure of their decision and had already made contact with SAMS in Brazil. After some initial difficulties, they were put in touch with Arthur and Gillian, an English couple involved in church planting there, who also facilitated adoptions through SAMS. Over the months, by telephone and email, the relationship developed into a strong friendship.

During the summer, the possibility arose of adopting an 18-month-old boy whose mother had died from AIDS. Before being released for adoption, he would need to have medical tests done for AIDS and other illnesses. Henry and Mary began to get excited again – perhaps this was the one God had for them. They paid for all the necessary health tests to be done and filled out a multiplicity of government forms; although many children needed adoption, they were not released easily, until it was certain that the adoption was in the child's best interests. There was a seemingly interminable wait before the case eventually came to court.

The health tests turned out to be clear, but the law in Brazil stated that Brazilian nationals had priority over foreigners in any adoption. Suddenly a Brazilian couple came forward to adopt the little boy they had hoped for. Henry and Mary saw the situation as a door firmly closed. They had a strong sense of God's leading and, while disappointed for themselves, they were glad the child had found a home. They believed that God was working in that court and knew clearly in their hearts that God did not want them to have this child.

The next child offered to them was a 7-year-old boy. They thought about it carefully, weighing up their desire for a child against the problems of uprooting him from his own background and culture. Introducing a 7-year-old into a foreign country with a new language and a whole different way of life would pose a huge challenge. They decided against it.

A year passed with no further developments and by the following summer they were aware that they were running out of time. Deciding to go to Brazil themselves during the summer holidays, they were dismayed to discover that all flights were fully booked. Twenty-fifth on the waiting list, they were not hopeful of obtaining a flight at a time they could go. One Sunday afternoon, relaxing in their garden, they suddenly wondered if there were any places available on package holidays to Brazil.

They made enquiries and discovered a travel firm that would allow them the flexibility to do their own thing in addition to the organised holiday. Before they realised what was happening, they had booked the holiday, including an extra flight in the middle for a five-day break with Arthur and Gillian, their contacts from SAMS. They did not really think that anything much would happen with the adoption process while they were in Brazil, but at least it would allow them to meet this couple who had been working with them through the process and who had become good friends.

Many months before, Mary had warned her headmaster that if they eventually succeeded in adopting a child, she would like to take a career break. He was very understanding, and she left for Brazil with the knowledge that if anything did work out for them, her job situation would be straightforward. They shared with their family the plans to meet Arthur and Gillian but emphasised that it was only a friendly meeting and perhaps another step along the journey. They were still focused on adopting a younger child but were very aware of the difficulties – time and opportunity were running out.

The first part of their holiday in Brazil was exciting, giving them the opportunity to see some of the country before catching the plane to where Arthur and Gillian lived. They were delight-ed to meet each other after all the long-distance phone calls and faxed messages. On that very first day, shortly after they met, Gillian said, 'I'm actually going to the government office now to discuss some adoptions that have gone through. Do you want to come?' Henry and Mary agreed to go along for the experience and were introduced to the social worker who was based there.

In the course of conversation the social worker suddenly remarked, 'There's a young boy who has just been released for adoption in the last few weeks. His mother has died and he is in an orphanage four hours' drive away.'

She showed Henry and Mary two photographs of a 9-year-old boy. They looked at the photographs, then at each other and, simultaneously, knew that all their carefully thought out reasons for adopting a younger child had been dispelled. They had talked about the dilemma that might arise if they had to choose between three or four children. In the event, the social worker only spoke to them about one child. They decided to go and see him.

It was not easy for foreigners to get into the orphanage. However, a couple in America had previously adopted five brothers from this particular orphanage and Arthur was taking a newspaper cutting about the story to show to staff at the orphanage.

'Come with me,' he said. 'We can go in together.'

The first obstacle was that the car refused to start and they began to think that maybe they were not meant to go at all. Eventually, however, the engine roared into life and they set off on the journey. As they approached the orphanage, Henry and Mary began to have some reservations about the visit, worried about what would happen if they decided not to adopt this child. They did not want him to know they were considering adoption in case it did not work out for some reason and he felt disappointed or rejected.

Keyed up with anticipation, they went inside with Arthur and the social worker. The boy had a dental appointment that day and was therefore not at school. The social worker introduced them to him as friends of Arthur, and when Arthur went off to see someone else, the social worker asked the child if he would show them the little farm attached to the orphanage.

Mary's memories of that day are crystal clear.

'The second we saw him, we looked at each other and we both knew without saying a word that we wanted to adopt him. As we went together to the farm, he communicated with enthusiasm and fun, despite our lack of Portuguese. We loved him immediately – our concern was that we might get too attached to him before we knew things were going to work out. He told us later that he had combed his hair that morning when he knew visitors were coming. He was putting on his best side for us, even though there was no spoken suggestion that we would even think of adopting him. It made me so sad that a child had to do that – he was worried that we might go away again without him.'

The three of them had a very special ten minutes together before joining the others for lunch. Mary recalls: 'While we were eating Henry looked up, caught the boy's eye across the table and winked at him. It was a very precious moment. We never doubted for a moment that this was the child for us and that the Lord had put everything in place. I had never been so sure of anything in my life. It was amazing because we'd had our hearts set on a younger child for so long. The worries about language and all the other adjustments just faded into insignificance.'

The social worker did not tell the boy of their decision in front of Henry and Mary but spoke to him later after they left. When she showed him on a map where Northern Ireland was, it seemed like a tiny dot compared to America. However, as he explained to Mary later, the geographical location was of no significance to him.

'I just wanted a mother and father; I didn't care where they lived.'

He had only been in the orphanage for a few months and because his mother had died, rather than having abandoned him, he did not have the feelings of rejection that some of the other children had. At the same time, more than anything else, he knew that he wanted a family of his own again.

At the end of the five days, Henry and Mary continued with their holiday, but now Mary was worried. What if someone else came and decided to adopt him before they managed to make all the necessary arrangements? Ireland was so far away. They returned home and arranged for Henry to have some time off work and for Mary to have her career break. Four weeks later, they returned to Brazil, where they had to stay until the requirements of Brazilian law were fulfilled.

Fortunately they were allowed to spend this time with their new son, who decided he would like to be called Patrick. The three of them stayed in a flat near the orphanage and Mary's heart went out to the other children there.

'We took sweets to share with the other children. One little boy wouldn't take the sweets or be in the photograph with the other children, because he wanted us to adopt him too. It was not possible because, as is often the case, his mother had left him in the orphanage and then disappeared, so there was no certificate allowing him to be adopted. It was heartbreaking to see so many others who would love to have been adopted but could not, because of the legal situation.'

Henry and Mary had to resist the temptation to spoil this adorable young boy who had come into their lives and who had already been through so much in his short life. However, they had made a conscious decision not to have a spoiled child who would not know the value of money. In some ways the period in Brazil was helpful in this regard, only having a certain amount of money with them and being restricted in what they could buy. Although there was no money involved in the adoption itself, they had to pay for translations of paperwork and for their accommodation in Brazil for several weeks. Patrick thought at first that his new parents would automatically buy him everything he wanted and became grumpy when he discovered this was not the case. Eventually, with the help of the Portuguese dictionary Mary conveyed to him the difficult lesson, 'Children cannot have everything they want.'

A vast amount of paperwork had to be waded through before Patrick finally belonged to them legally. Henry handled most of it, making sure everything was done in triplicate, not wanting anything to go wrong at the last minute. Eventually, after nine long weeks, it was all finalised. With glad hearts, hardly daring to believe that it was done, the three of them boarded the plane together for the journey back to Belfast and a new life together as a family.

Mary reflects on her feelings through the experience: 'I'm not proud of the thoughts and reactions I had when I was struggling with the issue of childlessness. I just thought, *How can I possibly cope?* Some people say, "My faith carried me through," but I have to confess that I didn't lean on God as much as I should have. Now I can see that Patrick was always God's plan for us, but I couldn't see how the plan was going to work out at the time. When you're in that situation and cannot do anything about it, you feel helpless and hopeless. Only someone who has experienced it can know what it is like; I still identify with any mother without a child – I know so well what she feels, what she's going through. The pain never totally goes away; you always feel second best as a person.

'I am still not the first to go and look at a new baby. When my niece was a baby, I enjoyed holding her and of course I love her, but there is still a little feeling at the back of my mind, that consciousness of having been denied the experience of giving birth. To a certain extent you bury your feelings but, whatever happens, you never really get over the sense of loss at not physically giving birth to your own child. Of course now, although I would love to have had the experience of the birth and the early days, if I had to choose between giving birth or having Patrick, I would choose Patrick every time. Patrick is definitely not second best, he is the best thing that could have happened to us. Meeting Patrick for the first time was indescribable, it was so wonderful. I would not have wanted anything to replace that.'

For many women praying fervently for a child, the anguished questions are often, 'What's wrong with me? Why does God answer someone else's prayer and not mine?' There is, of course, no answer to these questions. The problem of unanswered prayer goes much wider and deeper than prayer for healing or prayer for a child. If the God of love who sees and understands our pain is also the almighty God who can work miraculously when he chooses, then it is hard to understand and accept that he chooses not to answer our prayer in the way we would like. For Mary, the answer came in the form of Patrick; for others the answer is different. For all of us, we can know that although we cannot see the whole picture now, God's answer is not second best. One day we will see more clearly.

Now we see but a poor reflection as in a mirror; then we shall see face to face. Now I know in part; then I shall know fully, even as I am fully known.
1 Corinthians 13:12

5

Daddy's Bread

Ella watched as the policewoman patrolled the main street, hands tucked into her flak jacket, eyes constantly on the move, alert to anything that did not seem quite right, any unexpected move that might signal danger. She was being tailed by a male colleague, a few paces behind, watching her back. Ella's own job as an insurance clerk paled into routine insignificance as she contrasted it with the daily excitement and challenge of life in the Royal Ulster Constabulary. With two uncles in the police force, she knew something of the demands of life in the RUC in the early seventies and her goal in life was to be part of it.

The present Troubles had begun with the civil rights protests at the end of the 1960s, and the consequent reaction. The situation would dominate Irish history and politics for the next thirty years. In the seventies, the Troubles were at their height; Interpol figures showed that by 1983 Northern Ireland was the most dangerous place in the world to be a police officer.[6] Ella's parents, having no desire for their daughter to risk her life in the fight against terrorism, had resolutely refused to contemplate the possibility of her joining up.

Understanding though she was of their reservations, Ella decided she could not postpone the decision indefinitely. She sat the entrance examinations and was accepted for training, before going to break the news to her parents. At the age of 23, she left the cocoon of her safe, comfortable job and in June 1972 went into the RUC training depot in Enniskillen. Forty women were taken each year, ten on each quarterly intake. With forty-two men in her squad, Ella felt the ten women held a somewhat privileged position.

One month later, on 21 July, soon to be known as Bloody Friday, 22 bombs were planted in Belfast and in the resulting explosions 9 people were killed and a further 130 civilians injured. Ella's parents were distraught. When she came home for the weekend from Enniskillen, her father was clear.

'That's it. You're not going back.'

'Oh yes I am, Dad, I love it. It's what I want to do.' Ella was quietly determined.

Her first posting as a woman constable was to the RUC station in Dunmurry, just south of Belfast. The local headquarters for the area, it covered the well-known hotspots of Twinbrook and Andersonstown. Going out on foot patrol and driving police cars and Land Rovers alongside the men in her section was exciting and fun. Her main responsibilities, however, were offences regarding women and children; she was regularly called upon in cases of rape or flashers operating in the local parks.

Although she thoroughly enjoyed the varied nature of the job, Ella understood that it would not all be pleasant. Road accidents were often distressing and the so-called 'segment duty' at the security gates in Belfast was long and tiring. During the Troubles, the centre of towns and cities was closed to traffic, with all pedestrians required to have their baggage searched as they passed through security gates into the city centre. Police officers had to sacrifice rest days to carry out this duty, although it was a useful way of boosting their income.

In those pre-equality legislation days, it was felt that women were a liability out in Land Rovers on night duty, so although Ella was on call at night, she did not go out on the beat with the men. When on duty, however, she was called out most nights to deal with situations involving women, whether victim or suspect. In general, women officers were seen as a race apart and treated with respect by the men. Their smart dark skirt and jacket with crisp, white blouse and plain black shoes presented a very different image to the present day unisex uniform of trousers and boots.

The woman superintendent, based in Castlereagh RUC barracks in Belfast, was totally in charge of all woman police constables. A woman inspector and woman sergeant were in control of each division, with the sergeant visiting the local station every week and the inspector once a month. They inspected each woman constable's filed records and logbooks on these visits and checked with the duty sergeant that she was performing her duties properly. Any problem concerning a woman police officer would be referred to the woman inspector, who was responsible for her women and ruled matron-like over those in her charge.

A flurry of preparation in the local station regularly preceded the inspector's visit. Sweeping into Dunmurry police station one day, she eyed a uniform skirt hanging up in the office and demanded of the unfortunate police officer, 'Is that your hockey skirt?' Uniform skirts were supposed to be below the knee, not shortened to distract vulnerable males.

Ella often found herself dealing with girls caught up in the Troubles, perhaps trapped in the situation because of boyfriends. Parents sometimes had no idea their daughter was involved and Ella tried to be sensitive as she worked with the families. 'I loved every minute of it. I always tried to treat people the way I would have liked my own family to be treated. I found that if you treated people with respect, then they respected you in turn.'

As part of her regular duties, she helped to man road blocks, checking for stolen vehicles that could be used for car bombs or other terrorist activity. Alongside the British army stationed in the province, Ella's section carried out house searches in sensitive areas, looking for arms and ammunition. While these activities presented a certain amount of risk, she accepted them as the normal way of life for an RUC officer. She was living in the midst of the Troubles, but she had to live as normally as possible, even though the threat of violence was always at the back of her mind as a possibility. It was important to keep the balance between carrying on with life and being aware of the dangers.

In certain areas, it was commonplace for young people to stone police vehicles, calling for a steady nerve as she drove through the streets with stones bouncing off the Land Rover. If the police had been called in to help in a difficult situation, however, then everybody was pleasant. Reacting to the different facets of the job demanded understanding, discipline and self-control.

Sometimes her duties took her to the security wing of the local hospital, guarding people who had been injured because of their involvement in terrorist activity. Eight hours at a time with many of these patients allowed her to get to know them and gave her some insight into their situations. There were many reasons why people found themselves caught up in the Troubles and, conscious that she had only limited knowledge of the details of their lives, Ella decided she might as well be pleasant to everyone she guarded. One patient used to ask specifically for her, calling her 'the girl with the brown eyes'.

Ella enjoyed the excitement of the job, not knowing what a day would bring, and the sense of satisfaction in contributing to society. Looking back she marvels at how she loved it then, although she cannot imagine doing it now. 'From this distance I can understand my parents' fear and concern over my career choice. To a young person, it was an adventure, fulfilling and worthwhile. I had little concept at that stage of what my parents were going through.'

On the evening of 10 May 1974, two men from her section, Brian Bell and Malcolm Ross, went out on foot patrol as usual. Ella was supposed to go with them, but as she was called to a shoplifting case at the last minute, they went without her. A few minutes later they were on duty, standing at a crossroads, when a car drove up and within seconds they were both shot dead. The shooting was announced on the local radio station which had every policeman's wife in the area telephoning the station in terror to discover the identity of the victims. Staff at the police station could say nothing until the next of kin had been officially informed and the details released.

Ella went with the chief inspector to break the news to the wives. At first Ann Bell, who was expecting her second baby in September, thought Ella was there on a casual visit, as she would sometimes have called socially. As soon as she realised she was accompanied by the chief inspector, however, she deduced that this was no ordinary visit. Her anguish was painful to watch.

Margaret Ross, mother of two young sons, refused to believe that Malcolm was gone. Reality only filtered through as her church minister, family and friends all began to arrive at the house. Telling these young women that their husbands were dead was one of the most difficult duties Ella ever had to perform.

Recruitment into the force was boosted through the police cadets, where 16- to 18-year-olds were appointed to undergo training, with a view to becoming full-time members of the police force. In return for a salary, they attended the local further education college, and took part in a wide range of sporting activities, before moving to the Enniskillen depot to train as constables.

Three years after her appointment to Dunmurry, Ella was transferred to Lisburn as a cadet trainer. Entering in to this experience with enthusiasm, she travelled throughout Northern Ireland with the cadets, enjoying the outdoor life and varied activities – everything from mountain climbing and canoeing to hockey and swimming. Her career was as stimulating and fulfilling as she had dreamed it would be.

A year after moving to Lisburn she met John, an RUC constable based at a nearby station. John's work in the transport section took him all over the United Kingdom. Four years older than Ella, he had joined up in 1963, before the introduction of the 42-hour working week, doing 24-hour shifts, lying out behind hedges during the early Troubles, with no such thing as overtime pay. When Ella met him, his job involved the recovery of hijacked vehicles all over the country, often in high-risk situations, going into volatile border areas at midnight to pick up stolen cars or hijacked petrol lorries and drive them out under cover of darkness. He escorted building contractors bringing in their materials at night to police stations or army bases, because of the security risk.

Two years later, in 1978, John and Ella were married. Work commitments involved both of them being away from home during the week, working very anti-social hours, which they understood and adapted to. When their son, Richard, was born in February 1980, however, Ella realised that it was not feasible for her to continue, however much she loved the job. Women with children were not facilitated, unsociable hours were part of the job and she had no extended family around to help with childcare. Reluctantly, she handed in her notice.

Much as she loved her young son, staying at home with a little one was very different from being out there as part of the action. Suddenly Ella had more time to think about the dangers of John's job, although she had long accepted risk as a natural part of their life together. When she woke in the morning, it was with a sense of relief that the phone had not rung during the night – if anything bad had happened, she would have heard. In those days before mobile phones it was impossible to keep in touch when John was out on a job. Ella reflects, 'I was under stress as a policeman's wife, but I really felt it helped to have an understanding of the Troubles from the inside because of my experience as a policewoman. I often thought about women who did not have that familiarity with the situation, and wondered how they coped.'

Living under constant threat, all police officers had to keep their identity as secret as possible. They travelled to and from work in civilian clothes, wearing a coat over their uniform or keeping it in the police station and changing when they got there. John and Ella lived in a peaceful part of the country, where personal security was somewhat lower risk, but Ella knew that families in the town, for example, could not hang their police shirts outside on the clothesline with the rest of the washing. Only certain restaurants were safe for them to visit and John always positioned himself where he could watch the door and see anyone coming in.

One day in January 1983, when Richard was almost 3 years old, he was at playgroup as usual when he suddenly had a seizure. It seemed to be a one-off event, from which he recovered without any obvious side-effects. In October of that year he had another episode, which the doctors decided to investigate more thoroughly. Ella suffered with him as he underwent a brain scan and an excruciating lumbar puncture. Eventually they were given a worrying diagnosis of epilepsy; he would be on medication for the rest of his life. The treatment controlled it well, however, and he soon resumed the normal active life of a 3-year-old.

In April of that year, Ella and John were delighted at the birth of a baby daughter, Alyson. Their family was complete and happy, apart from the stresses of John's job, with which they had learned to live. Growing up in a pleasant rural situation, the children were shielded from the effects of the

Troubles. They were never taken into Belfast and in their quiet little country school they were almost oblivious to what was going on in other parts of the province. John and Ella were careful not to discuss anything to do with religious differences and never mentioned John's work while the children were around. Alyson and Richard knew their parents checked under the car every morning before driving it and were careful about opening the door at home until they knew who was there, but this was life as they had always known it and they assumed it was the norm for everyone. They had no idea what their father's job entailed, thinking he was a lorry driver because he brought the police lorry home at night.

Once, on a caravan holiday, a boy from a neighbouring caravan questioned Richard.

'What does your daddy do?'

'He's a lorry driver. What does yours do?'

'I'm not allowed to tell.'

Overhearing this exchange, Ella realised the family were involved in the security forces and suggested to the mother that the child be given a safer explanation for his father's occupation.

Ella knew she had to continually be careful about who she spoke to and what she said. Unknown to the children, John had a personal weapon, which was kept hidden in a hollow inside a cupboard when he was at home. At night he slept with it under his pillow. It was the normal way of life for RUC officers at the time.

In July 1987, John became unwell. A deep fatigue gripped him, which the doctor put down to stress and overwork in the RUC. A second opinion, however, and further tests, revealed that he had a heart condition called cardiomyopathy, which he may have had for some time, but was not helped by his stressful way of life. He needed open heart surgery.

In October, John had a mitral valve in his heart replaced. He went into hospital on Monday, had the operation on Tuesday, made a good recovery and Ella was delighted to bring him home again the following Monday. The valve was stainless steel and, disconcertingly, could be heard ticking like a clock. His body took some time to adjust and it was a year before he was able to return to work.

A trained mechanic by background, John was always fascinated by cars. During his year of convalescence, he had time to develop this interest and started to collect old cars, beginning with a Baby Austin as his first purchase. Unable to undertake any strenuous activity, he enjoyed tinkering with the cars and found in them a positive focus for the long months of recuperation. Ella, used to her creature comforts, would say to him, 'I hope I like these cars, because they have no radio and no heater.'

Soon, however, she also fell in love with the cars and it became a family hobby. They joined the vintage car club of which John's brother was already a member, and almost every Saturday packed the two children into a car and travelled to rallies all over the country. Ella became more and more involved, ending up as secretary of the car club. In August 1990, Ella's best friend Liz asked for the use of one of their cars for her wedding. It turned out to be the first of many weddings where the cars would feature.

Finally back on his feet, John returned to work. The following year, however, he was forced to acknowledge that he was having disquieting symptoms and reluctantly submitted to further investigations in hospital, which showed that his heart was once again struggling. One Saturday in February 1991, the doctors informed them that John was very seriously ill; his only hope was to have a heart transplant. He would have to be assessed at Papworth Hospital in Cambridge and go there for the operation. Without it he had perhaps six months to live, although there was no guarantee that he would even last that long.

Ella was devastated. It was questionable whether he would get the new heart in time and even then it was a very risky operation. She was 42 years old, and the children were 7 and 10. They had so much to look forward to together in the future. How could they cope without him? She spent the weekend in tears. John, however, was determinedly positive, focusing on the hope held out by the prospect of a transplant. When he got his new heart, it would be like a new engine in a car, he would be healthy again. John remained in the Royal Victoria Hospital in Belfast, with Ella visiting him every day. Most days she brought the children with her in the afternoon; he loved to see them and they brightened his day. Richard, old enough to realise the seriousness of his father's illness, was concerned about what was happening, but Alyson played happily in the ward. The hospital was not in a good area of the city, but Ella, more concerned for John than for her personal safety, used the hospital lift on her own at night, walked through the darkened car park and drove home without thinking about it. Only looking back later did she realise the risks she took.

As week followed week, John's assessment in Papworth was repeatedly postponed because of his condition. John, convinced there would be a miracle and that he would somehow get his new heart, continued to talk as if it was going to happen, but Ella could see him deteriorating and realised it was becoming less and less likely. As he became aware of the worsening situation, John wanted to keep the family's spirits up and refused to acknowledge his growing weakness. One evening, as he was unable even to do his usual Bible reading for himself, Ella read it to him before she left the hospital. As this became their normal practice, he would often preface it by saying, 'You won't have to do this when I get my new heart.'

While maintaining a positive front to Ella and the family, John quietly put in place all the practical arrangements necessary should he not recover. He sorted out the family finances and organised a grave in the cemetery beside the church which the family attended regularly. Every Sunday he said to Ella, 'Don't come in until you've been to church.' Their minister, Revd McConaghy, was a constant help and support both to John in hospital and the family at home.

'In the event of anything happening to me . . .' John began to say to Ella, prefacing his thoughts and wishes. He hoped Richard would be a mechanic, being practical like his father. 'Give Alyson a good education,' he said. 'Everything's there for you. Stay in the house as long as you can, but if it's too difficult, just move somewhere else.'

John's organs were deteriorating. He was very weak and gradually became confined to bed, only able to be moved with the aid of a hoist. For such an active man, the indignity of this was unbearable. He began to lapse in and out of consciousness. During one of the times he was unconscious, he could hear the family talking round his bed, although unable to communicate with them. When he recovered consciousness, he was able to tell them what he had heard, but he talked also of a brightness surrounding him, soft and light like cotton wool. He felt so content and peaceful that he had not wanted to come back.

Mary Angus had been a friend of John's since childhood, having attended the same Sunday school, Bible class and church with him over the years. Now working as a hospital chaplain, she became a great encouragement to him, listening, talking and praying with him every day. Once he surfaced, after having been unconscious for two days, to find her at his bedside. Looking at the cross she wore round her neck, he said, 'That's where I was, Mary. I was at the cross and met the Lord, but he sent me back.' The medical opinion was that physically he should have been gone, but his faith and positive outlook kept him going.

It was obvious he was not going to get well; it was a matter of struggling through each day. Ella comments, 'When you are in the situation, you deal with it and live each day as it comes. We had been used to doing that anyway in our work situation. Each day was a bonus, and some days were better than others.' Despite his growing weakness, John determinedly maintained his interest in the motoring world and every night insisted on looking at the advertisements of cars for sale in the Belfast Telegraph. These glimpses of the John she had known kept Ella going.

On the evening of the 18 April, he was sitting, propped up, watching television when Ella came in to see him. Because he had been so ill that week, Ella had been staying at night, sleeping in a nearby room, where the nurses could call her if there was any change. That night he seemed much better, but at quarter past six the following morning, the nurses came for her. 'Once we turn him now, that will probably be the end,' they said.

Ella recalls, 'I was with him as he just slipped away. Although I was heartbroken to watch him go, in a way it was a relief for him because he had suffered so much.'

Ella felt a sense of unreality. She tidied the room, gathered up everything she needed to take home and telephoned the undertaker.

'Who is with you?' he asked, when he realised she was speaking from the hospital.

'No one, I'm here on my own,' she replied.

She seemed to have a calm strength that lifted her above the situation and carried her through all the practical arrangements that had to be made. One of the nurses telephoned her brother and his wife, who went home with her to tell the children. Her parents had been staying with the children that week, and by

the time Ella arrived home, the rest of the family had gathered
there, along with Revd McConaghy.

Richard knew something was wrong, with so many people
in the house, but he was devastated when Ella actually told
him that his father had died. She would have done anything to
shield the children from this pain, but knew that they, like her,
had to go through it. Alyson at 7, did not fully understand and
wanted to go to school.

'Mummy's alright, she has everyone else here,' she said.

In the end a friend came and took her for the day. Although
not outwardly distressed in the same way as Richard, she was
subdued, playing for a while and then sitting quietly by herself as she tried to understand what was going on.

On the day John died, Mrs McConaghy, the minister's wife,
gave Ella a couple of verses from Isaiah 57:

> 'I have seen his ways, but I will heal him; I will guide him and
> restore comfort to him, creating praise on the lips of the mourn-
> ers in Israel. Peace, peace, to those far and near,' says the LORD.
> 'And I will heal them.' (Isaiah 57:18–19)

She stuck the verses into the front of the Bible she and John
had received on their wedding day, which she read from every
night. She says, 'I found that verse such a help that day and in
the days following. I always put it in a sympathy card now
when I am sending one to someone else.'

On the days leading up to the funeral, the house was busy with
friends coming to support Ella and the family. She was worried
about the funeral itself, not knowing in advance how she would
be able to cope. That morning, a neighbour came in and quoted
words to Ella which are sometimes seen on gravestones, and
which remained in her mind throughout the day: 'Thy purpose
Lord we cannot see, but all is well that's done by thee.'[7] While this
thought would have been difficult for some to take on board at

such a time, she had no sense of resentment towards God for taking John, or any feeling of being cheated out of the rest of her life with him. She accepted that somehow it was part of God's plan for them all. 'Above all I was glad he had made a commitment to the Lord and knew where he was going. That was the greatest comfort.'

Although entitled to a police funeral, John had made it clear he did not want one. Revd McConaghy and Mary Angus, who had supported them so faithfully during John's illness, conducted the service with a personal sensitivity which was very meaningful to Ella and the family. Alyson spent the day with a friend, while Richard accompanied Ella to the funeral. It was only at this stage that he discovered his father's real profession. Even then he protested, 'My daddy's not a policeman, Mummy.' There were too many factors for him to assimilate all at once.

To Ella, conscious only of the sea of faces in the church, much of the day was a blur. 'I had attended many police funerals over the years and I used to look at other young widows and wonder how they could possibly cope with what had happened. Yet it's amazing how you get strength when you need it. As I went through the motions of the funeral and all the activities surrounding it, I thought, *I'm doing this for John. I have to be sensible here.* And I was able to carry on.

'Apart from the fact that he was missing, it was almost like a party, a celebration. All his friends were there. It was only when I came home and sat down afterwards that it hit me. I found myself thinking how I would describe the day to John, until I suddenly realised he would never be there for me to talk to about anything again.'

John was buried on a Sunday. On the Monday morning it seemed to Ella that for the rest of the world everything was back to normal again, almost as if nothing had happened. She heard someone cutting their lawn nearby and realised that life was continuing around her. 'I had to light the fire and get on with my work in the house. The children had to be fed, taken to school and their after-school activities. My parents stayed for a week, but after that I had to get back to normality.' In recent years, Ella had been doing childminding at home, so she had to continue her commitment to the children, giving her a daily focus.

The following Sunday, Ella was back at church as usual. She looked forward to that regular Sunday pattern, gaining great strength from her attendance there. 'The Lord had something to say to me each time I went. It reminded me that I wasn't the only one to be bereaved and there was no point sitting in self-pity at home.'

She returned to all the church organisations she had been involved with before John's illness. The Girls' Brigade captain asked her to consider helping with the organisation, so she completed the training and became an officer. She continued in the car club, which developed into a lasting hobby and interest. Through it she made many friends, not only throughout Ireland but all over the United Kingdom, as she began travelling again to rallies and shows accompanied, of course, by the children.

Despite her determination to carry on living, Ella missed John constantly. The nagging pain of his absence was always with her. Although the children missed him too, their pain was different. Everything was new to them; their future was in front of them, while Ella's life had been tied up in her husband. 'The feeling of loss was like an indescribable pain in the pit of my stomach. The only way to deal with it was one day at a time, until eventually the pain eased. I kept busy, kept going out, and the days became weeks, the weeks became months, and the months became years. The difficult part is that people expect you to get over it; they don't want to listen to you complaining. Grief is a very lonely experience.'

Not wanting to upset their mother, the children did not cry when she was around, although Richard admits that he cried alone when he went to bed. Somehow, at the time, Alyson was led to believe her father would come back. She heard people saying things like 'You'll see him again' and 'He's in a better place' which, at the age of 7, she interpreted to mean that one day he would come back. When, four years later, she confronted the fact that this was not going to happen, she became very distressed and went through a delayed bereavement process. Ella says, 'It was a comfort to her at the time of her father's death to think it was not forever, and it helped me that she was not too upset, but it was wrong. She needed to be able to grieve with the rest of us.'

Despite her grief, Ella was conscious of a responsibility to make life as good as possible for the children. The family had been keen caravanners in Ireland and Europe since the children were little and Ella didn't think they would ever do it again after John became ill. A month after his death, however, she decided to face the challenge and drove the car and caravan to the coast for the weekend. Step by step, she was proving to herself that she could do things which she had relied on John to do in the past. The following year she pushed herself to take the children to Cyprus on holiday.

'Making decisions was always difficult; it was one area where I felt very alone, and yet I knew I had to do it. The only way was to get on with it and do the best I could in the situation.'

The little family of three became very close. It showed in simple things, such as the discussions over who sat beside Mummy in the front of the car. The rota for this was suddenly very important to them, always having been confined to the back before John died. Richard, at the age of 10, claimed he was the man of the house, taking very seriously the role of protecting his mother and sister.

As the year of John's death drew to a close, Ella organised a treat for the children – a trip to Belfast for the first time ever, to see the Christmas lights. Because of the Troubles, John had never allowed them to go into the city, and although the situation was a great deal calmer by 1991, Ella could not help feeling somewhat guilty. She found herself thinking, *If John knew I had these children in Belfast at Christmas, he'd turn in his grave.*

Ella had been out of the workplace for years while the children were growing up, but she knew she needed to get back to work now that John was gone. She gave herself a year at home, before taking a computer course at the local further education college. When the children were both at high school, she looked for a job where she could work mornings only and found it in the office of the *Church of Ireland Gazette*, where she has worked happily ever since.

The RUC benevolent fund was a real blessing to the family immediately following John's death and throughout the ensuing years. Each year Ella, as a police widow, was offered a weekend away, a week in an apartment on the North Coast or a week in London. The children had the opportunity to go on activity holidays for police widows' children. Richard was reluctant to go without Ella, but Alyson went on a wide variety of holidays throughout the United Kingdom and Europe. An education grant was provided for her right through to university level. Ella says, 'We have been very well looked after. I have no complaints, only I don't have John.'

As John had hoped, Alyson went to university and obtained a first class degree in Fine and Applied Art, followed by a Masters degree. Her grief over her father's death, however, lingered on. Part of her primary degree, a project which she called 'Daddy's Bread', was covered by the BBC in a piece entitled, *Aly McLoughlin Uses Her Loaf*. In the project, Alyson looked back to the time when she and Richard, as young children, would stay at home with their father on a Saturday while Ella played hockey. Ella always left a pot of soup or stew ready for the family at home and John would get an unsliced loaf of bread which he cut up and buttered for them to eat with the soup. The children have referred to this particular type of loaf ever since as 'Daddy's Bread'. For her degree project, sponsored by a well-known bakery with a year's supply of bread, Alyson assembled 798 of their bread bags, the exact number of weeks since her father had died. On film, she picked out the bags one by one, until in the end, unable to find her father, she kicked off her shoe in disgust against the wall. Her exhibition created great interest and she was thrilled to have the opportunity to explain her artistic thought processes to so many, but the emotion of it all left her drained for a week afterwards.

Richard remained on medication for his epilepsy, but did not allow the condition to deter him from anything he wanted to do. He became an enthusiastic member of the Boys' Brigade, completing the top awards and becoming an officer; he was a good swimmer, played football and enjoyed outdoor pursuits. At 16, he started work as a joiner, which eventually developed into a thriving business.

Ella says, 'His driving licence is renewed every three years, he rides one of those horrible scramblers and he runs his own business.' When she hears him complaining about the amount of work in hand, she looks at him and thinks, *Darling, thirty years ago you were a sick wee baby; you are a fortunate boy to be where you are today.* Now things have turned full circle, and Richard is building a house for the son of John's best friend.

Ella says, 'We were a one-parent family and it hasn't always been easy, but I feel so fortunate that the children have grown up into the mature, caring adults they are. Richard gets mad when he hears negative comments about one-parent families. We stayed very close and supported each other all through the years.'

The children's wedding days were difficult without John – although in each case the time leading up to it was worse than the day itself. Ella had many tears and thoughts before the weddings and worried about how they would all deal with it on the day. In the end she found that the rehearsal was the time she was most upset, dealing with the emotion of John's absence at such a significant event. On the day itself, just as she had found many years earlier at his funeral, she was carried along by the atmosphere of the occasion and the support of friends and family. In his wedding day speech, Richard reminded the guests of the importance his father had always placed on the children being well behaved and of his repeated instruction each time they left the house, 'Remember, when you're out, people see your manners, not your brains.'

'What makes me sad now,' Ella says, 'is that he's not here to see how well the children turned out. John was 37 when Richard was born and he was beginning to think he would never have children. He idolised them. He would have loved his grandchildren so much.'

Ella still recalls clearly John's words to her in the hospital. 'In the event of anything happening me, don't be sitting in the corner crying all day. When you feel the time is right, get up and get on with life and if you meet someone else and the spark is there, and you have a chance at happiness, take it. But put a flower on the grave on Sunday when you're at church.'

Ella did eventually meet someone else, but the grave has never been without a flower. John's positive influence lives on through his family. Ella is grateful for all they had together. She says: 'He was courageous, he was positive, he was an inspiration, he was a good man.'

It is an enviable epitaph, but Ella is oblivious to her own portrayal of these qualities over the years – her courage and optimism in the face of difficulty, inspiring her children to follow all that is good, setting an example that is now reaching the third generation. The mourning and despair of the past have been turned into gladness and praise.

To bestow on them a crown of beauty instead of ashes, the oil of gladness instead of mourning, and a garment of praise instead of a spirit of despair.
Isaiah 61:3

6

For Better, For Worse

'Excuse me, could I borrow your Italian phrasebook?'

As a chat-up line, it was not very original, but it gave Jill the opportunity to get into conversation with the good-looking fellow hitchhiker she had spotted on the Trieste beach. He conveniently turned out to be a zoology student from London, where Jill was in teacher training. On their return home, the friendship developed into a serious relationship, and eventually marriage. After graduation, they worked for eighteen months in Somerset before moving to Hull to allow Mike to pursue his PhD studies.

Four years after their wedding, they were given the news that they could not have children. Rather than trying to explain when parents and family members made meaningful comments or asked leading questions about the situation, Jill clammed up, unable to talk about it to anyone other than Mike. Together, however, they decided to explore the possibility of adopting a child who would not otherwise have a home. Submitting to the necessary extensive procedures, they were accepted as suitable adoptive parents and settled down to an indefinite wait.

When the news eventually came, it was very sudden; they were going to be parents to a six-week-old baby boy. The lady who had fostered him for the first weeks of his life brought him to their house and Jill could not believe this beautiful little boy was theirs.

'It was as if she had just given us an amazing gift. As I felt his soft weight in my arms, I remember thinking how little he was. Despite all the preparatory interviews, I felt very unprepared to look after him. That first day, I proudly took him out for a walk in a borrowed pram. It was only when he had been crying for a while that I realised he might be hungry and took him home to feed him.'

Before adopting Christopher, Jill had been undergoing fertility treatment in Leeds hospital. Unbelievably, shortly after he came to them, she discovered she was pregnant – with twins. After years of thinking she would never have children, she now had one baby and was expecting two more!

On completion of Mike's studies, he was offered a lecturing post at Nairobi University, with the Overseas Development Agency. Deciding to accept the initial two-year contract, Jill and Mike moved to Kenya in 1973. Mike went in February to sort out accommodation and Jill, now four months pregnant, followed a month later with Christopher. They moved into their house and began to adjust to life in a very different culture. Jill took Christopher along to a playgroup where a group of expatriate mothers befriended this new arrival and, unknown to her, prayed for her. She took up a part-time teaching job and started to feel more at home.

Barely two months after arriving in Nairobi, Jill woke up one morning in intense pain. Not knowing what was happening, Mike ran to get the doctor who lived next door. There was nothing he could do, however. Jill had a miscarriage and lost the twins. Still comparatively new to the country, feeling lost and homesick, Jill and Mike were devastated. Aware only of the pain of her grief, not knowing what to do, Jill appreciated the mothers from the playgroup who rallied round to support and care for her and help her through the dark days.

Somehow, Mike and Jill came through that difficult time and settled into life in Nairobi. The sadness of losing the twins still lingered, but Christopher demanded their care and attention and provided a lively distraction. By the time the initial two-year contract came to an end, they were enjoying life in Kenya. Jill was teaching in a lovely school; they had made good friends; they were revelling in the outdoor lifestyle, the wonderful weather, the beautiful scenery. As Christopher grew a little older they enjoyed swimming together in the warm sunshine and exploring Kenya's amazing game parks. They decided to renew their contract for another two years.

During one school holiday, they set out with some friends to make the long journey to Masai Mara Game Park. Christopher and his friend Graeme were having fun together in the back of the camper van, when suddenly it ploughed into sand and turned over. Mike emerged relatively uninjured but the others were less fortunate. Christopher had multiple fractures, Graeme had a nasty head injury and Jill had numerous injuries, including a broken collar bone. Unconscious, she knew nothing about the accident until she woke up in Nairobi Hospital, where her first thought was for the rest of the family. Gently they broke the news. Mike was fine, Graeme was ill but recovering but Christopher, the centre of their world, had gone. He had died in hospital, just before she recovered consciousness.

Jill remained in hospital for a few days, recovering from her physical injuries but stunned by Christopher's death. The pastor of a local church came and prayed with them. Other friends visited and tried to bring some comfort. A few of them talked about Jesus but Jill and Mike had no clue what they were talking about. One of the playgroup leaders, a nurse who had lost a child herself, kindly took them into her home and cared for them for a few days after they came out of hospital. Jill felt frozen and detached from all that was going on around her.

'All I was conscious of was that losing Christopher was the most dreadful thing that could happen to me. I remember seeing his coffin being put into the grave and the feeling of him being torn away from me. We had waited for him for so long and loved him so much. I could not accept that it had happened.'

She arrived home from hospital to discover that Christopher's sand pit had disappeared from the front of the house. Mike, wanting to relieve her of this constant reminder of happier times, had given it away to friends. The empty space turned the knife in her heart once more. So many memories were tied up with that sand pit; Christopher had spent hours playing in it with his friends. Somehow its removal symbolised the permanence of his loss. She could not comprehend what had happened and how life could possibly continue.

Distraught and angry, not knowing where to turn, Jill went back to England, where her mother gathered her up and looked after her. Inundated with letters from friends, she was unable to open any of them. In Nairobi, Mike struggled on alone. He had gone there with such high hopes, to a new job, with a wife and child, and twins on the way. Now he was left without any of them, filled with grief and loneliness. Looking back, Jill realises, 'It must have been a dreadful time for him. I couldn't help him and I was so far away. I don't know how he survived.'

In England, Jill struggled to come to terms with Christopher's death. The questions would follow her throughout her life. 'I still don't understand why we had to lose him. I never went back to the grave – I couldn't face it. There seemed to be no point. He was not there; he lived on in my thoughts. It's still a very sore, very tender spot. I know that God was able to bring good out of the situation but that does not explain why it happened. I often wonder what Christopher would be doing now, if he had lived. I have so many questions but God is loving and just; he knows all the answers.'

Back at the Leeds hospital, Jill accepted further fertility treatment. 'I prayed vaguely that this God I barely knew would do something. I had lost three children. He had to give me a reason for living – anything.' Mike came to England on a home visit and, amazingly, Jill managed to become pregnant again. When Mike returned to Nairobi, she stayed on in England so that the hospital could monitor her progress.

One very snowy day, Jill drove through treacherous conditions to the hospital for her regular check-up. Struggling to find a parking space, she rushed in, late for her appointment, to discover that her blood pressure was raised. She was immediately admitted to hospital, where she remained for the rest of the pregnancy.

The boredom of the hospital day was only occasionally relieved by visits from friends, as most of them lived far from Leeds. Jill began to look forward to the regular visits from the hospital chaplain, enjoying the stimulation of their conversations; something about the presence of this older lady made a deep impression on her. As a child, Jill had attended a Catholic school and knew some Bible stories, but she had no idea about the concept of personal faith. What this lady was saying about Christianity, however, seemed to make sense. It sounded as though Jesus could answer some deep-rooted need in her life; she spent many hours thinking about it.

Boredom suddenly switched to anxiety when a scan showed that rather than one child, she was again expecting twins. This was bad news. Given her history, she was sure she would lose them again. A short time later, a further scan showed an unexpected shape on the screen; unbelievably, there seemed to be a third baby. Another doctor came running over to do the scan again, but it was true. She had already failed to carry twins to term so there was little chance that triplets would survive.

'My first phone call to Mike in Nairobi was joyful, full of excitement about the new baby; the second, telling him about twins, was much more subdued. The third was to let him know we were now expecting three babies and frankly I was very worried. With his usual dry humour, he told me not to call again!'

With Mike's return to England in April, they were able to communicate face to face, free from the restrictions of the uncertain telephone system. Jill talked to him about her search for faith, although she was still fairly hazy about what it all meant. She felt, however, that God held the key to what she was looking for in life.

Around six o'clock one evening, Mike left the hospital to go for a walk in a nearby park. Suddenly Jill's waters broke and she realised the babies were about to be born, six weeks early. Frantically she rang the bell for someone to get Mike back. She did not want him to come all the way from Kenya and then not be around for the birth.

The staff calmed her down and managed to contact Mike. By half past seven, he was there, reassuring Jill that all was well. As the hospital had never had a triplet birth before, the medical staff wanted all the trainee doctors to be present, but were less keen to have Mike there. Jill insisted, however, and in the end they allowed him to stay to see a little girl born first, complete with a head of black hair, followed by her two brothers. All three were born in the space of four minutes and taken immediately to intensive care. They each weighed two and a half pounds.

Shortly after the birth, Jill developed a blood clot, causing such agony that she was convinced she was dying. Again there was a frantic phone call for Mike to come. He waited while doctors operated quickly and his wife and children all fought for their lives. The operation was successful and slowly Jill began to recover, although it was some time before she was strong enough to hold the babies. Somehow, however, they seemed to grow and thrive. As soon as possible, she moved out of the noisy ward to a bed and breakfast nearby, but for the first couple of weeks she was so full of medication that she hardly saw the children. Five weeks later, she had recovered sufficiently to take them home to her mother. By this time Mike had had to return to Nairobi and Jill waited impatiently in England until the children reached the required five and a half pounds in weight to be allowed to fly.

En route to Nairobi at last, Jill, her mother and an air hostess shared the task of caring for the children, so that each one had an adult's full attention. The three little babies lay lined up sideways in one carrycot in the front seat of the plane. The nine-hour flight was delayed by a further eight hours, causing no little anxiety about the milk supply for the babies, but eventually, to everyone's relief, they arrived safely in Nairobi. Friends had been wonderful, rallying round to help Mike prepare for the arrival of Jill and the children. One couple in particular looked after and supported them as they settled back into life in Nairobi with the triplets.

Mike and Jill began to meet with a group of young couples their own age, some of whom were clear about their Christian faith and others who, like Mike and Jill, were struggling with doubts and questions. They met regularly for a meal, followed by discussion of issues relating to the Christian faith. Gradually all the thoughts and questions of recent years began to make sense to Jill and Mike. After about a year and a half, everyone attending the group had become a committed Christian and they began to encourage each other to grow in their faith and to share that faith with their children.

Jill reflects, 'Looking back, I worked through lots of issues, especially my deep anger over the loss of Christopher. I think ultimately God used the situation to bring us to faith. At that time there were a number of young wives in Nairobi struggling to have babies and other mums who had lost children. It helped us all as we began to share our experiences, and our faith, with each other.'

The triplets grew up in Nairobi, thriving in the relaxed, outdoor life of Kenya. Mike continued to lecture in the university for six years before moving into consultancy work. The family moved north to a school in the hill country, when Jill was offered a teaching post there. By this stage Mike was travelling backwards and forwards to Uganda, so the Kenyan highlands was a good location. They enjoyed four years in this happy school before the children's education necessitated a return to England.

Jill did not want to end up acting as chauffeur for three teenagers, so for their relocation they looked for a small market town where the triplets could access most places on foot and could board at school if necessary when Mike was working overseas. When they finally settled in Louth in Lincolnshire, finding a church where the triplets would all feel comfortable was high on the priority list.

This was more problematic than they had imagined. They discovered a number of other teenagers in the town, all looking for a church that catered for their particular needs. Eventually, a group of parents of teenage children decided to start a service themselves, which was totally teenager orientated and lasted throughout the triplets' teenage years until they went to university. The leaders encouraged the young people to get involved in outreach activities, took them to Spring Harvest and focused on doing anything that would suit their age group and keep them active in their Christian faith.

Once the children went to university, Jill was free to shut up the house in Louth and join Mike wherever his consultancy work took him. Involved in environmental impact assessment, he worked with engineering firms operating mainly in Africa but also Brazil and China. Trips back to the UK allowed them to keep in touch with friends and family, although it was always somewhat traumatic having to say goodbye again.

Over the next four years, the triplets completed their university courses and moved into full-time employment in various parts of the UK. Jill was offered another teaching post in Kenya, which would allow her closure on her teaching career there. She liked the idea of moving back into a mission setting. Mike would work on the environmental management of the complex. At the end of August 2004 they arrived in Kenya and settled into a lovely little house on the school compound. Jill was delighted to be back, although it demanded all her concentration and energy to teach GCSE courses during the day, do preparation at night and cope with boarding duties in between.

Two months later, Mike woke Jill early one Sunday morning. Distressed and disorientated, he asked her repeatedly, 'Where am I? Why am I here?' He knew who Jill was, but seemed to recognise nothing else around him. When he eventually fell asleep again, Jill got dressed and went out to see if there was anyone around who could help. The compound was quiet and peaceful, disturbed only by the morning song of birds in the surrounding shrubs as thy welcomed the rising sun. A vestige of early morning mist draped itself round the nearby hills like a soft, white scarf. The compound itself was deserted; everyone was enjoying a slower start to the day. Reluctant to disturb their Sunday morning calm, Jill went back to the house where Mike was now sitting up in bed again demanding, 'What's happening? What's the matter with me? Why am I here?' Really worried now, Jill telephoned the school nurse, who came immediately.

The nurse, whom Mike knew well, appeared to be a stranger to him. Agitated and anxious, he fired constant questions at Jill.

'Who is that? Why is the squash racquet sitting there against the wall? What time is it?'

Jill attempted to present an unruffled exterior and calm him down as best she could. Meanwhile the nurse, aware that something was very wrong, telephoned Nairobi hospital and made an appointment for the following day. Tired out from all the questioning, Mike kept falling asleep but in the afternoon Jill encouraged him to go out for a short walk round the compound. Although physically able to walk, he had no recognition of his surroundings, which frightened them even more.

It was difficult to arrange cover for Jill in the school at such short notice and to find a driver to take them to Nairobi the next day. The three-hour journey, over appalling roads, was a nightmare for Jill, trying to reassure Mike while wondering what was happening to him and what the outcome would be. When they eventually arrived in Nairobi, the doctors seemed baffled and over the next few days carried out a wide variety of tests in an attempt to get to the root of the problem. Jill and Mike returned to school, with the promise that results would be sent through as soon as possible.

A few days later, they received the promised report – Mike seemed to be exhibiting the symptoms of Transient Global Amnesia, although normally in such cases short-term memory would return fairly quickly. As this was not happening in Mike's case, the recommendation was that he go to London or South Africa for further investigations. As they had been to South Africa on holiday and were familiar with the situation there, they decided it was the easier option. It took time, however, to organise the trip and Jill found it very stressful trying to cope with Mike's disorientation while she sorted out frustrating travel details. Eventually everything was in place and they managed to get out of Nairobi airport and onto the flight to Cape Town.

In Cape Town the doctor examined Mike at length, repeating the tests that had been done in Nairobi and confirming the diagnosis they had received there. They stayed in a lovely Bed and Breakfast and managed to have a very pleasant time despite the circumstances. Their son, Stuart, who happened to be in Johannesburg on a work assignment, flew to Cape Town to be with them, which was a great support to Jill. She was recovering from the initial shock and learning to come to terms with the situation while they waited for the doctors to find some way to help.

The prognosis was not hopeful. They flew back to Kenya with the news that it was unlikely there would be any further progress in Mike's recovery and that medically little could be done for him. It was obvious that he could no longer work, so they would have to leave Kenya and return to England. Their house at home was on a long-term let, however, and with the recent pleasant experience in South Africa fresh in their minds, they decided to spend the next six months there, travelling round the country in a camper van.

This was an amazing experience: they enjoyed the stunning scenery, took long walks together and Jill found an outlet for her creativity in embroidery and painting. They had plenty of people contact at campsites and spent Christmas and New Year with friends. However, the reality of Mike's illness remained with them, a dark cloud hovering over this extended holiday idyll. One day he left the camper van to walk to the toilet block and did not return. The park where they were staying was vast, with wooded areas, wild animals wandering through from time to time and few other campers. Jill was very frightened until she eventually managed to find him, but it was a wake-up call for her, bringing home the implications of his situation.

While they were in South Africa they visited the doctor in Cape Town again, who confirmed the original diagnosis and suggested they go to Addenbrooke's hospital in Cambridge, where extensive research had been done into the condition.

Back in England, they followed this advice and arranged for Mike to go to Addenbrooke's for tests. The diagnosis this time was slightly different. The consensus was that Mike's symptoms pointed to encephalitis, an inflammation of the brain as a result of infection or because his immune system, for some reason, had attacked the tissue of the brain by mistake. Devastatingly, there was no treatment the medical profession could offer; all they could do was make some suggestions on how to handle the problems caused by memory loss.

'No change,' said the doctor regretfully. 'There will be no change. Basically it's a matter of living with it as best you can.'

By this stage, pooling the knowledge from her teaching background and from talking to others, Jill was already developing a strategy to enable them to cope.

At first there was a sense of novelty in the challenge of trying to maintain life and relationships with such a disability. Jill was determined to be positive, to draw up strategies, to make the very best of the situation. She felt they could cope with it together, especially with the support of family, friends and church. They tried not to let it stop them doing what they wanted to do. They kept in touch with friends and family. They went on an extended trip to visit their daughter, Sarah, and her husband, Paul, who were now working in Sri Lanka. They enjoyed a happy family time together there, visiting new places, meeting new friends, revelling in the warm sunshine and outdoor life that they loved.

Under normal conditions at home in England, however, Jill could not escape the realisation of just how difficult life was going to be. The implications of Mike's disability were far-reaching. He could cope without Jill in the house for short periods of time, but for most of the time he needed her around. The reality was that neither of them would ever be in paid employment again. Mike, who used to take responsibility for the entire administration involved in running the household, had lost all ability to deal with money. He could no longer cope with anything technical, including the computer. Jill found she had to shoulder total responsibility for everything around the home and for the organisation of their life.

Used to supervising major governmental projects all over the world, Mike was now unable to problem solve in even the most basic situation. He found it a challenge to prepare a meal or work on the allotment. He could manage to do these tasks with help and direction but was not naturally a gardener or a cook and did not find them innately fulfilling. Jill did everything with him so that he had the help he needed to feel some sense of accomplishment. They visited the library regularly and he came back armed with huge novels, but his concentration only lasted a short time. With little short-term memory, he could not carry the thread of what he was reading in his mind. He was unable to play board games that involved numbers or do anything that required counting, although word-based games were important and enjoyable. He was physically able to drive but had no recognition of his surroundings so he could only drive if there was someone with him.

Getting up in the morning was very difficult; facing each new day was a major challenge. He knew what he could not do. He understood that he was not the person he had been and being around those with whom he used to work now made him feel inadequate, underlining what he had lost. He shied away from situations he found frightening, especially if it involved groups where he would be unable to remember who was who.

The disability affected his faith. It was hard to pray when he could not remember what the issues were. They continued to go to church together, although Jill was unsure how much Mike was taking in, as he was unable to remember or discuss it afterwards. He did not like staying to talk to anyone after the service, as the large crowd in the church hall was not a comfortable situation for him. Because he found it difficult to speak about his faith, Jill did not know what he was feeling or how much he understood about the concept of faith in this new dimension in which he was now living. She wondered if he felt God was to blame for the situation. At the same time, she held on to her faith in a God of love who understood what was going on and trusted that the Creator God had his own way of communicating with a disabled mind.

In Africa, Mike had been a keen windsurfer and at first Jill went regularly with him to the lake near their home, enabling him to continue that interest. He found it increasingly difficult, however, to remember what to do. Used to the warm Indian Ocean, he found the local lake a poor substitute. The boards were more difficult for him to manage, the weather and the water were cold, the lake was boring and the wind fickle. When Mike talked about windsurfing he grew very enthusiastic, remembering how wonderful it had been on the East African coast and forgetting that the experience in England was less than satisfactory. It broke Jill's heart to hear him talking to his friends as if he was still surfing regularly in Africa.

When they were alone at home, communication was difficult. Mike tended to be very quiet for much of the time, only talking if he really had to. 'My head is empty,' was his explanation. This was difficult for the naturally talkative and outgoing Jill to deal with. 'When I talked, I continued to think about what I had said afterwards and I expected Mike to be thinking about it too and to be forming a reply, but he forgot what I had said almost immediately, so there was no follow-up comment. Unless his reply was instantaneous, the thread of the dialogue was lost. It was very frustrating trying to hold a conversation.'

Jill began to realise how deeply the difficulty in communication and the changes in Mike's personality were affecting their relationship. Because Mike was unaware, or did not remember, that she was doing everything, he did not express any appreciation. As far as he was concerned, everything just happened. Although understanding Mike's problem, Jill still found the lack of encouragement very difficult, especially as she would normally have had constant support and encouragement from her colleagues at work. Mike had no concept of what she also had lost or of her personal and emotional needs in the situation.

Although Jill was glad to help him, she needed to feel appreciated. Their daughter Sarah's response was to buy Mike a diary and work with him, putting in reminders on different weeks to buy Jill flowers one week, chocolates another, to say thank you for her help.

Conscious of his disability, Mike would often become very depressed and dissolve into tears when he thought about the life he had lost. Trying to support Mike and get him through the difficult days, Jill would then have her own times of despair. Eager to make use of any help available, she had a few sessions with a counsellor, but found it of limited value when the counsellor could not relate to her framework as a Christian.

She found the house too large to look after. When they originally bought it, the plan was that Mike would deal with the decorating and practical upkeep, but now that was impossible for him. Sometimes Jill became very stressed because he was so dependent on her for everything. She would wake up in the night in a panic, full of worry and fear.

'I know it's not right to panic. God wants us to trust him. My worrying is not showing trust in him, so it's something I really have to work on. The future has to take care of itself. We have to remember that God is our father and he knows the limit of our ability to handle the situation. So many times when we have been at the end of the road, he has stepped into the situation and intervened. I need to call those times to mind when I start to panic.'

At the beginning of 2008, Jill decided they had grieved enough; they would have to make a new start and look ahead.

'Count your blessings' would become her mantra, as she constantly reminded herself to appreciate all that was good in life. They organised regular visits to Jill's mother down in the south of England, along with trips to each of their three children. Sarah and Paul now lived in London and they enjoyed combining a visit to them with a day out in the city.

Although unable to commit to a permanent job, Jill felt she needed some stimulation outside the house. She volunteered with the Citizens' Advice Bureau locally, finding fulfilment in helping others for two mornings each week. Leaving Mike at home, however, demanded some creative thinking. She put up a whiteboard in the kitchen and, before leaving in the morning, she would write on it where she was, what time she would be back, what there was to eat, what Mike could do while she was away. While she was out of the house, she kept in touch with him by phone to check that all was well. Her work with the Citizens' Advice Bureau gave her a sense of fulfilment outside the home, and put her own problems into perspective. She joined a painting group and an art appreciation class. She stayed involved with various groups at church, including the music group and prayer group and enjoyed helping to make banners.

Although all this helped Jill's own mental state and ability to cope, it did not help her relationship with Mike; she was still very aware of the gap in their relationship. When she came home, the time that would formerly have been filled with discussion about what she had been doing was now a vacuum. She realised it was unfair to expect Mike to be concerned about how her morning had been, when he could not remember where she had gone, or to give feedback or appreciation of her latest painting when he was unaware of the effort and time involved. She had to keep reminding herself that that kind of interaction would not happen any more.

A holiday alone with Mike was no longer a holiday for her and so she began to plan holidays where they could both enjoy being with friends. It was good to spend time with people who had known Mike before his illness, as they respected him for the person they had always known him to be and could talk to him about events in the past. Jill was very conscious that those who had only known him since his illness had less than half the picture. As Mike was able to cope with four round a table at mealtimes, she began to organise small dinner parties that kept them in touch with friends in a manageable way. She discovered that he talked better when she was not there, as he tended to leave the talking to her if she was in the room.

They developed a routine for the week, realising they had to pace themselves. She arranged for him to play tennis twice a week and he also enjoyed table tennis. Each month they went on a long walk, organised by the University of the Third Age. The local branch of this self-help organisation for those no longer in full-time employment gave them the opportunity to make friends with others who were in similar circumstances to themselves. Mike enjoyed listening to classical music and they were fortunate to have regular concerts taking place locally. As they realised how much he could still do, they tried to keep focused on the positives.

A breakthrough came when they discovered the opportunity for him to help in 'Get Talking', a local project teaching English as a foreign language. The teacher welcomed Mike's participation as one of the volunteers, helping the students with their set tasks. It seemed to give him a sense of fulfilment, perhaps linking back in his mind to his former work with university students.

Jill realises, however, that the onus for organising all Mike's activities rests with her. 'Life is a case of problem solving. I spend much of my time trying to give him tasks he can do and then praising him and letting him know he has achieved something. The things he can do now are so trivial compared to what he used to do, that he often feels useless. I try not to put him in a situation where he will fail but rather where friends will support him. I try to prepare well beforehand so that folk know his situation and needs as far as possible.

'Mike is still loving and caring but he's very different now. We live with this ongoing problem. I tend not to talk to him as much as I used to, because it is so difficult to find a hook that he can latch on to. Instead of just saying "I met Betty today" (the lady who lives next door but one) I have to explain who she is and how we know her. We can't discuss books or newspaper articles, as he doesn't read. It has affected the whole way we relate to each other. The buck stops with me and there are still days when I come home and the loo is overflowing or something has gone wrong and I think, *I can't cope with any more.* Then I consciously remember all the good things that we have and I ask myself, *Why am I complaining?*

'I do fight a constant battle against depression. Sometimes I just have to pray it through and realise the situation is not going to go away. I try to praise my way out of the hole. Being part of the worship group in church really helps to keep my spirits up and I find those Wednesday and Sunday times with them very inspirational. A number of studies have shown that singing with others reduces depression and increases feelings of well-being, and this is much more the case when we are praising God together.

'When I feel bad that Mike does not express any thanks or appreciation for food that is thoughtfully prepared, I wonder sometimes if that is how God feels. He has given us so much and yet we can ignore all his blessings and be depressed about the difficulties of our situation. We have little reason to complain really. We are so blessed. I could be a widow but Mike is still alive, physically healthy, loving and fun, even though he is different from the Mike I used to know. I am aware of the truth of the old Persian proverb, "I murmured that I had no shoes, until I met a man who had no feet." [18]

Jill is full of admiration for the way Mike has coped with his great loss. 'He tries hard to remain positive, he still has his sense of humour and often comes out with a relevant and amusing pun. He has lost so much and it must take so much strength to face life each morning. I thank God for each day I have with Mike and for his strength of character which will not let this disability conquer his spirit.'

Jill has a strong conviction that she should use what she has been given, so that rather than wasting the pain she has been through, she can receive God's comfort and pass it on to others. She quotes 2 Corinthians 1:3–5: 'Praise be to the God and Father of our Lord Jesus Christ, the Father of compassion and the God of all comfort, who comforts us in all our troubles, so that we can comfort those in any trouble with the comfort we ourselves have received from God. For just as the sufferings of Christ flow over into our lives, so also through Christ our comfort overflows.'

'Everyone has some kind of challenge to deal with and I'm conscious that God has equipped me to help those in particular situations because of what I've been through myself – whether it's a young couple struggling to have children, those going through the adoption process, parents who have lost a child or, more recently, those who care for a disabled partner. I have quite an affinity now with couples where one of the partners has dementia and I have a number of friends who need support in this way. It helps to keep my own situation in perspective.

'As to the future, I don't know what to think. I couldn't even go down the road of wondering what would happen if I died before Mike. He would not be able to live alone. When the children were little, we had no godparents for them – we had too many children all at once to try and organise it and we felt God would sort it out and look after them. I feel the same now with Mike. God will keep him in his care. All I need to do is keep trusting him for the future and thanking him for all the good things in the present.'

Because of the Lord's great love we are not consumed, for his compassions never fail. They are new every morning; great is your faithfulness.
Lamentations 3:22–23

7

My Son, My Son

It was a fairytale wedding. The sun shone as the horse-drawn open carriage drew up outside the picturesque country church. Carol shook out the embroidered skirt of her heavy satin dress and took her father's proffered arm as he helped her down onto the red carpet. From the doorway of the building, she glimpsed her groom standing tall by the altar, flanked by best man and groomsman, all three pristine in their Royal Air Force uniforms. The organ music changed, a murmur ran round the church and Carol's whole being thrilled as her husband-to-be turned slightly and looked down the aisle to watch her approaching on her father's arm. It was hard to believe it was actually happening: at last, after all the planning, she and Andrew were about to become husband and wife. Life in the forces would pose its own challenges, but they were facing it together, with God's help.

Married life began in Singapore. After adjusting to the climate, life was full and interesting for Carol and Andrew. Two years later, they were delighted to be expecting their first child. Baby Jack arrived unexpectedly early, cheating Andrew, back in the UK on a training course, of those first magical moments of his life. Carol felt somewhat unprepared emotionally for his sudden arrival, and the speed of it all left her in a state of shock, wondering how well she would be able to care for this new baby.

Missing Andrew and her family far away in Scotland, she felt inadequate and abandoned. She knew she had plenty of friends around and good medical care readily available but during those first days she was homesick for Scotland and the reassuring presence of her parents.

As soon as Andrew managed to get back, however, he was enthralled with his new son. 'I'll be able to take him fishing!' he exclaimed with glee, undeterred by the fact that he had never fished in his life. As they drove home from hospital, Carol oscillated between overwhelming love for the baby in the back of the car and a disconcerting sense of responsibility for this new little life. Unfazed by Carol's apprehension about their ability to cope, Andrew's joy and pride in his young son grew rather than diminished as the days went by and together the new parents made happy plans for their future as a family.

Despite Carol's concerns, Jack was a well-behaved baby and there were no interrupted nights after the first three months, no pacing the floors, even when he was teething. A very sound sleeper, he took all the changes in his young life in his stride. When he was 4 months old, the family moved back to Scotland, where his delighted grandparents were able to be more involved with their young grandson. The only cloud on the horizon was a succession of bad colds which plagued him, one after the other, leaving him grumpy while he was ill. These usually responded to antibiotics but life was miserable for everyone while he was unwell. Carol came to accept this and realised philosophically that all children had illnesses of various sorts; learning to cope with the accompanying ill-humour was all part of being a parent.

Three years later, the family suddenly expanded when twin girls were born. This time Carol had much more support with all her family around her. Andrew and Carol did all they could to prepare Jack for the arrival of his siblings, including bringing him a present from his sisters on the day they came home from hospital. Jack, however, was not to be persuaded that these intruders were a good idea. He was jealous of the attention they demanded and one day, when Carol's attention was elsewhere, bit one of them on the toe. Carol struggled to know how to cope with an unhappy toddler whose world had been turned upside down and a crying baby who was in pain. It was an ongoing dilemma and the relationship between the children remained difficult for some time, testing Carol's patience and ingenuity.

Ten months after the twins were born, the family moved to Germany. Jack was going through a difficult phase, still intensely jealous of his sisters and suffering from sinus problems. With Andrew often away on exercises, Carol once more missed the family support that she'd had at home. She struggled to know how to help Jack, physically and emotionally. Eventually, the physical problems eased when he had his tonsils removed which, in turn, to Carol's great relief, helped him feel better about life in general.

As Jack grew, he became independent and strong willed. An active and inquisitive child, he had a habit of wandering off on his own, giving Carol some heart-stopping moments, especially when shopping or travelling. Once he disappeared on an Italian beach, causing great consternation until they found him playing happily on his own, not far from where they had missed him.

Germany offered an active social life for both parents and children. Jack was regularly invited to friends' birthday parties but a ritual developed which frustrated and puzzled Carol each time it happened. He would be ready to go to a party, dressed for the occasion and present in hand, when just before leaving the house, he decided he did not want to go. Later, Carol discovered the reason for his reluctance was his failure to win any of the games at the parties. Embarrassed and self-conscious, his sensitive nature led him to withdraw from the situation.

He became very emotionally involved when watching cartoons on television or at the cinema. One night, wondering why he was particularly upset and unable to sleep, Carol discovered that his school class had been shown a film based on animal cartoon characters, but the message of the film had affected him deeply. For many years the family would tease him about his reaction to the film, but looking back now, Carol acknowledges that as parents they were not tuned into his sensitivities at that early age.

Education was always a dilemma for families in the forces. In the early years, Jack adapted well to the various schools he attended, but as Andrew's job necessitated moving around, the children did not have much time to settle in each place. On the fourth change of school, there were a number of problems and Carol and Andrew were forced to face the issue. It was not fair to keep moving the children from school to school; they had to make a choice. One possibility was for Carol to set up home with the children and remain with them in one place so that they could attend school there, which would mean being apart from Andrew for extended periods of time. The other choice was to send the children to boarding school.

Some heart-searching months later, just after Jack's ninth birthday, Carol and Andrew decided on the second option. They picked a school in Scotland, close to family so that there would be nearby support and ease of access for weekend visits. Jack, having been regaled with thrilling stories about boarding school from friends, was keen to embark on this new adventure. He was proud to don his uniform for the first time and very excited to be progressing to boarding school status. The parting took more out of Carol than it did out of Jack. Heartbroken inside, she tried not to quench her young son's happy anticipation of an independent life.

The first half of the term was very difficult. Once the novelty had worn off, Jack was homesick, missing his parents and sisters greatly. Later, Carol would discover that, like many new boys, he was bullied during the first term. At the end of the first half-term break, he was a little tearful the night before his return, but the next morning there was no trace of tears as he prepared for the journey back to school. Once there, he settled in very well and built up a good circle of friends with whom he remained close for the next ten years of school life. Like all young people, he looked forward to the holidays with happy anticipation, but having spent some time at home, he was quite glad to go back to school and rejoin his friends. School, rather than an ever-changing home environment, seemed to provide the stability he needed during his formative years

In each of the different places they lived, Carol and Andrew became actively involved in their local church, and encouraged their children to join the Christian Union at boarding school. During Andrew's overseas posting, Jack's grandfather took him as a young teenager to communicant classes at the local church, where he made a personal decision to follow Christ. In senior school, however, Christian Union conflicted with rugby training and was dropped from his schedule. Alongside rugby, Jack was involved in athletics and, following in his father's footsteps, the Air Cadets, all of which he loved. Somehow his faith became secondary and never seemed to grow.

Carol and Andrew did not face the usual parental hassles of ensuring that homework was done, coursework completed, exams revised for. When they heard their friends agonising over what time their teenagers should be expected home after a night out with friends, they realised that in their case, for much of the year, many of these problems were the responsibility of the school; there was little occasion for conflict or confrontation on most of the issues which beset parents with teenage children. While the children were at secondary school, the girls now also boarding, Andrew was posted back to Scotland, allowing them to spend much more time together as a family. Jack seemed to have settled down and enjoyed his time at school, being appointed a school prefect in his final year.

He enjoyed regular weekends at home, giving Carol the opportunity to spoil him a little and, far from being a rebellious teenager, he was happy to attend church with the family on Sunday. The relationship between the children had improved by this time and each year until Jack was 18, the family enjoyed going on holiday together. With Andrew away from home so much, Jack and Andrew did not do many of the father and son activities of which Andrew had originally dreamed, but the time they did have together was happy and peaceful.

Leaving school for university in London brought wider choices about priorities and lifestyle. At first, Jack attended a local church and Carol and Andrew encouraged him to join the university Christian Union, but to their intense disappointment his Christian faith seemed to take a back seat as his involvement in various student activities on the campus grew and the responsibilities of leadership provided him with a sense of fulfilment. From time to time he mentioned a few casual girlfriends, but Carol and Andrew were never introduced to any of them and gathered that none of them was of lasting significance.

On graduation, Jack was offered a job in the management of the university campus. For one who had enjoyed university life so much, this was a dream come true. One day, shortly after accepting this post, he telephoned Carol to warn her that he was bringing a girlfriend home to meet them. The prospect of the first official visit with a girl caused Carol's mind to buzz in speculation, not just about the girl, but about the significance of their visit to Scotland. Meeting them at the airport, she was very impressed by this lovely, outgoing girl, with her open, attractive personality. She had very clear ideas about her future career, without being arrogant, and she and Jack seemed to get on well together as a couple, with their many shared interests. Carol found herself thinking, *If this is the one, she'll be very acceptable!* One year later, Jack and Wendy were married on a beautiful sunny day, with all their family and friends present to celebrate with them.

The young couple did not come to Scotland often, but each time they did come, Carol was very thankful that they had such a good relationship and that things were going well for them. During their third year of marriage, Wendy's birthday was approaching when Carol said casually to Jack on the phone one day, 'I must get Wendy's birthday present.' He brushed the comment aside saying, 'I wouldn't worry about it,' which Carol thought a slightly strange response.

A month later, Jack sat down to talk seriously to his parents.

'I've got some news for you,' he said. 'Wendy and I are split-ting up.'

Carol felt in total shock. She had had no inkling that any-thing was amiss in the relationship. Desperately she hoped that even if they separated, they would perhaps get back together again. Maybe counselling would help.

She recalls, 'I felt such pain at the thought of them separat-ing and at the depth of hurt they must be feeling; my heart was breaking for them. My constant prayer was that God would work in their lives and that they would be able to repair the relationship, whatever the difficulties. We encouraged them to attend a local Alpha Course, but they didn't take up the sug-gestion. I felt so helpless, standing on the sidelines, unable to help. As parents, we always want to fix things for our children. I was unable to do anything to fix this.'

After six months, it became obvious that there was going to be no resolution and divorce proceedings started. Before they finally separated, one of the twins met up with Jack and Wendy in Yorkshire, where they were then living. She returned to Scotland, reporting that they were still good friends; they had just developed different interests in life with different career goals and felt they were no longer compatible. They had decided to part now, while there were no children involved, rather than leave it until later when it might be more complicated and painful.

Carol was heartbroken. 'We never saw Wendy again. I wrote to wish her all the best and tell her how devastated I was to lose the relationship we had with her. It was so much like bereavement. She sent back a lovely card saying that she would always be friends with Jack and that there were no hard feelings or bitterness. I just couldn't take it in. How could such a wonderful relationship be over? Why did God not answer our prayers? There seemed to be no answer to the questions.'

Jack rented an apartment with some friends and tried to adjust to living a single life again. The breakup affected him deeply, leaving him withdrawn and depressed, struggling to maintain an outward façade of calm in the face of inner turmoil. He continued to visit his parents in Scotland from time to time and gradually began to focus again on his career. Carol hoped that, with time, he would recover emotionally and find a new sense of hope and direction in life.

A year after the break-up, Carol and Andrew went to York to visit him, staying in a hotel and meeting up with him in the evening. Earlier in the day he had been to the house where Wendy was living, to clear out some of his remaining belongings from the garage. When they met for a meal, he seemed very upset, which Carol attributed to the fact that he was going through a further stage of the marriage breakup, realising again the finality of it all. He had brought some of his former wedding gifts to give to his parents.

'Are you sure you don't want to hold on to these things? They might be useful if you decided to get married again,' said Carol.

'That's not likely,' he replied.

Carol did not respond to this negative remark. Perhaps with time life would seem more positive. At the end of the meal, she left the men to finish their coffee together while she went to find the Ladies.

Once they were on their own, Andrew, realising that Jack was unusually distressed, decided he needed to address the issue more directly.

'Are you trying to tell us something?' he asked.

'Yes,' said Jack. 'I'm gay. I've decided that I have to face up to my sexuality.'

Andrew was stunned. He was saved from the need to reply by Carol's return to the table, oblivious to the revelation that had just taken place. Andrew paid the bill and they went to the theatre together as planned, Carol thinking the men unusually quiet. This marriage break-up was hard for everyone to come to terms with, but as there was nothing she could do to help the situation, she was going to try and enjoy the evening, regardless of the atmosphere. Andrew, meanwhile, felt totally detached from what was going on around him. His mind was in turmoil, knowing that Jack still had to tell Carol. From the theatre they went back to the hotel, where they ordered drinks and sat talking. Suddenly, Jack broke down, reducing Carol to tears also. She suffered with him, as she thought of all the hurt he had gone through since the break-up.

Hesitantly, Andrew said, 'Carol, Jack has something to tell you.'

As she looked at him questioningly, he spoke the words that she never thought she would hear.

'Mum, I'm gay. I don't want to be like this, but I have to face up to what I am inside. I have to do what is right for me.'

Shock and disbelief left her bewildered. While she had been attributing his distress to the loss of his marriage, all along it had been something totally different and unforeseen.

Carol worked for an organisation that occasionally dealt with legislation to do with sexual orientation. Suddenly, after all the theory, she was faced with the reality. Yet this was a reality that seemed totally unreal because it touched her personally, in a way she had never imagined.

This is my son, she kept saying to herself, trying to take it in, as she looked at his distressed face, so like his father's. *He is telling us he's gay.*

She tried to keep calm and not become emotional, despite the pounding of her heart. Thoughts raced through her mind. She believed the Bible taught that any sexual relationship outside of marriage between a man and a woman fell short of God's plan.[9] But this was not an objective situation: she was a mother, this was her son. She thought of the differentiation between sexual practice and the orientation itself.

He is telling us about his orientation, not practice, she told herself. *Don't overreact.* She struggled to find her voice, knowing she had to say something, speaking as if through a haze.

'Jack, whatever the situation, you are our son and that's the most important thing. You know what your father and I believe. But we will always love you and always be there for you.'

Appreciating his parents' measured response, Jack was relieved to be able to talk about it at last.

'I know it's not the way I have been brought up. If Wendy and I had not had problems, I would have continued in the marriage, but I have met a few gay men – one of them a close friend of Wendy's – and they are all just ordinary people, doing normal jobs, living normal lives but with a gay partner. I've met them and seen their lifestyle. I see that this is the way I am.'

As they continued to chat together, Carol tried to carry on as normal, despite the churning of her emotions. They said goodnight to Jack at the bus he was catching, turned to walk away and finally she broke down for the first time. *I have lost my son because of this*, was the only thought in her mind. She cried all the way back to the hotel. As they talked together there, Carol sobbed, 'The only help we have in this is God. We can't tell anyone else. God is the only answer.'

They spent a sleepless night. The next day, Sunday, dawned as though nothing had changed. They had arranged to meet friends at a church in the city that they had wanted to visit for some time. A few months previously, when they visited Jack, they had been unable to find the church, despite driving in circles for a long time. This time they made sure they had proper directions and managed to meet up with their friends. As the service progressed, Carol realised that God had ordained that they were there on that particular day. The sermon was totally relevant to their situation – it could not have been more appropriate. It was as if God reached down and delivered the message directly to her heart.

The minister spoke from Romans 8:28, 'And we know that in all things God works for the good of those who love him, who have been called according to his purpose,' pointing out that God uses all that happens to us, not to bring about an end to our pain, but to refine us and make us more like himself. Later in the chapter is the question, 'If God is for us, who can be against us?' Carol left the church that morning with the peaceful assurance that God knew all about the situation, that he was in control, that he was sovereign and would somehow work everything out for good in a spiritual sense.

That night they returned home to Scotland and immediately faced the question of what they should do. They decided they could not tell their relatives, especially the older generation, who would find it painfully incomprehensible. Unsure how people would react, and wanting to protect Jack, they decided to keep it from friends also. They were feeling their way; they needed to know the best way to deal with the situation. Carol telephoned a large London church with various support networks, but found limited help. There appeared to be nothing available in York that could be of help to Jack either. She checked the Internet but much of the support seemed to be based in America. There were some helpful articles from a parent's point of view but they offered no local links in the UK. She thought grimly, *I really don't know the best way of dealing with this but we're just going to have to get through it on our own.*

The next day Carol was back at work.

'Did you have a lovely weekend?' asked her colleagues, knowing she had been in England.

'Yes, thank you,' she replied automatically. Inside she was screaming *No! It's been the worst weekend of my life. If I had just heard that my son had a terminal illness, I could have shared it and everyone would have offered me sympathy and support, but I cannot talk about this.*

Somehow Carol stumbled through that week, feeling physically sick at times as her body reacted to the emotional upheaval. The twins came to visit and revealed that Jack had told them about the situation when they had visited him a few weeks earlier. They had been positive and supportive and encouraged him to tell Carol and Andrew. 'They'll be OK about it,' they had told him. Being 'OK about it' was all very well on the outside, but it did not ease the pain in Carol's heart. Things were far from 'OK' inside. She grieved for her son and for the isolation, loneliness and pain she felt lay ahead for him.

The following Sunday morning found Carol and Andrew back in their local church, where they were both very actively involved. The sermon that Sunday encouraged the church family to be there for each other, loving and supporting each other. For that to work, however, it was essential to be willing to share and be open with each other. Carol felt once again that the message was for them.

'I think we should tell Tom and Jane about it,' she said to Andrew. They had known Tom, their church leader, and his wife for many years and had a solid, trusting relationship with them.

'I'm not sure,' was Andrew's response. He did not know how to talk about it to anyone. That afternoon Tom telephoned.

'Why don't you come round later for coffee and a chat? We haven't done that for a while.'

Carol felt clearly that God was nudging them to share what they were going through.

It was not easy, but as they spent time with their friends that evening, they were able to share the whole story with someone else for the first time. With the chance to talk about it came a sense of release, as they poured out all their conflicting feelings of love and pain. Tom and Jane were kind and caring, acknowledging their hurt and loving them through it. Before they went home, the four friends prayed together, Tom asking that they would know God's peace in their hearts and his strength and wisdom for the days ahead. Carol and Andrew left feeling tremendously supported and encouraged. The situation had not changed but they did not have to face it alone; they were members of a family who could support and pray for one another, and walk through it together.

Tom and Jane did some research and eventually put Carol in touch with True Freedom Trust,[10] a UK-based organisation offering support not only to gay and lesbian Christians struggling with their sexuality, but also to their parents and friends. A few days later, Carol plucked up the courage to call the telephone number on the literature. An understanding gentleman listened as she talked through the situation. He replied, 'I've heard this story many times before. Just continue to love your son. We will send you some literature that might be helpful. If

Jack wants to get in touch with us directly that is fine, we'll be glad to help him in any way we can, but in the meantime you will have the literature to give you some guidance on dealing with everything.'

Carol discovered that this organisation, founded by Christians with a gay orientation, had a clear stated basis of faith and produced a quarterly newsletter, including stories from those who were working through the implications of their sexuality. Accepting the Bible's teaching that anyone who is unmarried, whether homosexual or heterosexual, should refrain from sex outside marriage, their message was that a sexual relationship is not a necessary part of life, that we should accept our sexuality but allow God to work through it. They also accepted that there were alternative viewpoints concerning homosexuality and acknowledged the right of individuals to choose how they live their lives before God. Carol and Andrew found this organisation most helpful in coming to terms with the whole situation.

They also put Carol in touch with another mother in Scotland who was dealing with similar issues. This couple's son had been at boarding school when they worked as missionaries overseas so, as they talked, the two mothers could identify with much of the other's story. They found they were facing the same question – in a Christian community, who do you tell? Carol found it very encouraging to be able to talk to a mother in a similar situation, coming from a Christian perspective.

On one of their visits to Jack, Carol passed on some of the literature to him. Unable to articulate clearly all she wanted to say face to face, she wrote him a letter clarifying her feelings on the whole issue. She did not want to pressurise him to follow any particular route, but she did want him to be aware of the information that this organisation offered. Jack accepted it without comment. Whether he followed it up or not, she felt

slightly better that he at least had the information and a telephone number if he wanted to use it.

Carol's initial fear that she would lose her son did not materi-
alise. She and Andrew continued to have the usual contact
with him when they went to visit him in York and enjoyed
welcoming him home for family events. He continued to be
the caring and understanding person they had always known,
sensitive to the feelings of his parents and grandparents and
keen to maintain the good relationship he had with them all.

'Nothing seems to have changed on the surface when we
talk together,' says Carol, 'and yet I know that underneath,
things have changed fundamentally.' For a while Jack lived
with a male partner in York. Although Carol and Andrew met
him, Carol found it difficult to visit them together in their
home and so tended to meet up with Jack on his own. When
he returned to Scotland to visit, for example at Christmas, he
came by himself.

Looking back, Carol says, 'I don't know if that was the right
way to deal with it or not, but it was the only way I could cope
at the time. I know other gay young people have refused to go
home unless their parents accepted their partner also. At least
we were spared that dilemma. Jack didn't put us in a con-
frontational situation like that. The fact that we managed to
keep our relationship with him was an answer to prayer in
itself. It probably helped that we were not dealing with it on a
day-to-day basis. Sometimes it was almost possible to forget
that the situation existed and then someone would ask about
Jack and, knowing about the break-up of his marriage, say,
"Maybe he will find someone else." I found those comments
difficult to deal with and still do, even though he is no longer
with his male partner.'

Carol tries to look at the positives in Jack's life. His career is
progressing well and he seems content to have set up house by

himself. But she worries that life will be lonely for him and that he will miss out on the joys of normal family life. She can see how taken he is with his nieces and nephews and knows he would have made a great father. Carol's daily prayer is that he will come to know Christ in a real way and, with God's Holy Spirit working in his heart, he will know how to lead his life in a way that is fulfilling to him and acceptable to God. All she can do is to keep loving him and praying for him and then stand back and trust in the power of prayer. She believes deeply that an omnipotent God has the power to change lives.

'Jack knows how we feel,' she says. 'In 1 Peter 4:15 being a meddler is mentioned alongside murder and thieving. I see one application of meddling as Christians telling non-Christians how to live their lives. We can tell them that they need Christ, but we can't demand that they live a Christian life when they are not Christians. I don't need to tell Jack how we feel – he knows. My prayer is that God will use this whole situation in our lives to refine us, and also that God will one day work in Jack's life in such a way that people will look at him and say, "Look at what God is doing in this man's life." Because of that hope, I don't despair. Pain comes to all our lives but we don't need to wallow in self-pity and misery. God is in control of it all. I cling to God and his promises and continue to trust my son to his all-encompassing care.'

And we know that in all things God works for the good of those who love him, who have been called according to his purpose.
Romans 8:28

8

To Love and To Cherish

'Become a teacher. You will always find a job as a teacher, whether you marry or not, and you'll earn enough to support yourself.'

Eileen mulled over her father's advice. She had dreamed of going to university to read History or English, but that dream was beginning to seem more and more unlikely. Her other interest was music: she played the violin and piano. Perhaps teaching music would be a viable career? In the late nineteen thirties, options were limited for a young woman from a south London working-class family, even one with Eileen's bright intelligence.

Eileen stayed on at school, her sixth form years dominated by the Second World War, to which her brother would be conscripted like all the other young men his age. The whole school was sent out of London because of the bombing. After two uncomfortable and unpleasant years of being billeted on people who did not particularly want school evacuees, it was a relief to be able to return home to her family, despite the continued bombing.

At the age of 18, she was accepted by the Royal College of Music in London, and for the next three years, lived at home and travelled daily to college. Her student years were inevitably coloured by the experience of living in wartime London, having to adjust to air raids and the resulting havoc, sleeping in a cramped 'Morrison' shelter which took up much of the space in the ground floor living room, accepting food and clothing rationing and the restriction of evening activities by the 'blackout'. This effectively meant that social life at college was non-existent, the students' main concern after lectures being to get back safely to their homes before dark. The student body in those years was mainly female, as most men over eighteen had been conscripted.

It says a lot for the College that it continued to function at all. In Eileen's very last week there, while taking her final examinations in the summer of 1944, a flying bomb cut out overhead. The entire room of students dived under their desks onto the floor as they waited for the inevitable blast. Fortunately, it missed the College, hitting the park beyond. Once the bomb had exploded, they returned to answering the interrupted questions.

Graduating successfully, Eileen found a job as a music teacher in rural Yorkshire, giving her much needed respite from London, providing her first salary and allowing her time to think about her growing interest in a young man whom she had met a couple of years before.

In 1943, one of her brother's friends had turned up at Eileen's London home to say goodbye before leaving for the war. Fred had just been conscripted into the RAF, halfway through his English Literature studies at Cambridge University. Academically gifted, a great debater with an almost photographic memory, he and Eileen struck up an immediate rapport and they kept in touch by letter until his demobilisation in 1946, when he returned to his studies in Cambridge. As soon as they met up again, they realised that their friendship was developing into a more serious relationship and they began to think about marriage.

The year between the summers of 1947 and 1948 proved an important time for them. Fred took a teaching post in Sussex for the year, while Eileen continued her music teaching, now in Surrey. They used their weekends and school holidays to meet up. Neither of them had ever been in a relationship like this before and it was both a delight and a challenge to begin to get to know not only each other but also themselves at a much deeper level. They wanted to talk endlessly about everything, and found they were both asking similar questions. Fred's war years had been very different from Eileen's but left him with the same sense of anger she felt at the ripping apart of their world in those years between 1939 and 1945. They found huge satisfaction in talking with each other about their experiences during the war, their expectations for the future and their understanding of the Christian faith. Fred's incisive mind rebelled against any ideology that he considered had not been clearly thought through. They tried to make sense of Fred's parents' marriage breakdown that had resulted in him being estranged from his father.

They talked about what they hoped for in their marriage, beginning with what they wanted for the wedding service – no impractical long white dress for Eileen, but a beautiful silk day dress that she would wear till it fell to pieces; no hesitating promises, repeated phrase by phrase after the officiating clergyman, but vows to be memorised and spoken from the heart. Those vows made in the presence of God were to carry them through the next fifty-two years and prove a great source of strength in all that lay ahead. They both wanted to be married in church and the commitment of a Christian marriage.

In his last year in school, Fred had decided to 'try out' Christianity and was confirmed as a member of the Anglican Church before leaving for university at the age of 17. This step was taken with many questions and uncertainties still in his mind about what kind of God was really being described in the seventeenth-century language of the Creed he had learned for confirmation. He had looked seriously at Marxism as an answer to the huge problems of the world, but came to see Jesus as the true answer to the needs of the human heart. He felt strongly that it should be possible to talk about God in everyday language and preferred modern translations of the Bible to the old Authorised Version.

Eileen had attended Sunday services with her parents or her grandfather from the time she went to secondary school. She liked the atmosphere in the beautiful Anglican Church building nearby and enjoyed the music led by the choir and organ. As she grew older, it made sense to her that God had chosen to teach us about himself through Jesus and the Bible, although she struggled with questions about the power of evil in life as she saw it.

As she and Fred began to talk about what they believed, he was the one who challenged her intellectually in his search for God. They tried to look more deeply into their faith – they read the Bible through, discovered commentaries and Christian books. Together they wrestled with the issues and led each other to the point where they agreed that if the reality of God was accepted, then this faith had to be of very practical importance in their lives, beginning with their marriage service.

Having achieved a first from Cambridge in 1947, with the offer of staying on to do a doctorate in Linguistics, Fred decided that rather than pursue the possibility of a promising academic career, he would commit himself to teaching in a pioneering school for African boys in Kenya, then still a British colony. He had seen deprivation in the places to which he had been sent in the war and had become convinced of the great need for teachers in other parts of the world. He had met and been inspired by Carey Francis, who had gone to Kenya with the Church Missionary Society and was now the headmaster of a school there. Although once labelled 'Red Fred', Fred saw Jesus Christ as the great revolutionary who could change lives and he had no illusions about the cost of Christian discipleship. After all, Jesus had said, 'Take up your cross . . . and follow me.'

Eileen considered going off to Africa with Fred a great adventure, although it was hard for her parents to let their only daughter go to a foreign land. Initially ignorant about Kenya as a country, she tried to learn all she could about this British colony and the six million African people, made up of many different tribal communities. As she read about Kenya's political history, she realised that the geographical boundaries had been drawn up as a result of the infamous 'Congress of Berlin' in 1884, when the leaders of the European nations had divided up the middle of Africa to add to their empires. Kenya had become a British protectorate in 1895 and crown colony in 1920. The millions of Africans affected had no idea what was happening at the time. Fred and Eileen both found themselves critical of the idea of 'empire', which they had been taught at school was good, not only for Britain but also good for all the countries taken over by the British.

Although just 16 when the Second World War began, Fred and Eileen had understood that in order to resist Germany's attempt to dominate first Europe and then the world, the whole British nation needed to be mobilised to fight for survival. The idea of resisting domination by others was easy for them to understand and the domination of other countries by their own country hard to accept. In 1947, India declared its independence of British rule, and inevitably other British colonies would follow. So they were very interested to see what they should find in Kenya.

In 1948, travel to Kenya meant a long sea-voyage, as civil air flights were only just being established. As Eileen had anticipated, it did indeed prove to be a great adventure. For the first four years, Fred was Head of English at Alliance Boys' High School, about fourteen miles outside Nairobi, where Carey Francis was Headmaster. Fred and Eileen were attracted by the ethos of the school, founded by an alliance of several Christian churches, attempting to uphold what were seen as basic Christian principles and to put them into practice on the ground. Not tied to any narrow sectarian structure, the school took boys from all churches and none. Fred and Eileen realised, however, soon after reaching Kenya, that the Christian faith had been brought there within the context of colonialism and that raised a number of questions.

They found Alliance High School an astonishing place in which to live and work. A fairly small staff worked devotedly to teach and look after an extremely intelligent student body, admitted by selective examination from all over the country. There was never enough money, but Carey was a totally committed headmaster, who knew every student personally and tried to visit their homes in the school holidays. Extremely intelligent, formerly a mathematics lecturer at Cambridge University but with a great grasp of many subjects, he was strongly motivated by his Christian faith. He was a brilliant teacher and clear communicator, who always looked for the very best staff he could find, believing that his students should have the best teaching possible.

As he was about the same age as Eileen's father, her first reaction to him was one of respect and even fear because of his strictness, but she came to like and admire him as she realised his fairness and integrity. He was looking to the future, when his students would be in charge of their own country and would need the best education they could get to do so. He remained a friend to Eileen and Fred for the rest of his life. When he died suddenly in 1966, over a thousand mourners attended his funeral service.

Eileen had not planned to teach when they went to Kenya, wanting to get used to being a wife in a new situation and then hoping to start a family. Hit by an unexpected teacher shortage, however, Carey Francis invited her to join the staff and

Eileen picked up her career as a teacher again, first in the boys'
school and then in the new Alliance Girls' High School, widen-
ing her scope beyond music to include English and religious
instruction.

The hunger they found in their African pupils for education
was mind-blowing. Secondary education was seen as a rare
prize by young Africans, who hoped it would open otherwise
closed doors for them. Outside the classroom, Fred and Eileen
emulated Carey Francis' example and set out to get to know
the students personally, inviting them to their home for tea and
buns on Saturdays, and visiting them in their homes, mostly in
rural villages, in the holidays. Living among the Kikuyu people, they learned all they could about their traditions and
began to learn their language. They felt their mental horizons
expanding as they met with another culture and way of life.

As the school day was highly organised and staff were
involved with the total life of the school, what social life the
staff had was mainly with each other. Carey Francis regularly
invited staff to have supper with him, and Fred and Eileen got
together with others to eat and socialise. They enjoyed walking around the area outside the school, got to know missionaries in the Kikuyu area and gradually made other friends
further afield. Every Saturday the boys organised their own
Saturday night entertainment which could be quite riotous but
gave them a chance to let off steam. As Eileen began to hear
African music, she was fascinated by its spontaneity, rhythmic
complexity and vitality. She was in charge of the school choir
and was proud when they won the shield at a choir competi-
tion held in Nairobi. The young Kenyans were natural musi-
cians and had a gift of improvisation which she did not have,
her classical music training tying her too tightly to the rules of
Western music.

In 1952, despite Carey Francis' hope that Fred and Eileen
would continue at Alliance, Fred was appointed Supervisor of

Protestant-sponsored primary schools across the district, eventually responsible for 133 schools. This meant a move to live at Kabete Girls' School, where Eileen became Headmistress. In this primary boarding school, started by the Church Missionary Society, she had the opportunity to shape the lives of 150 young girls who knew that if they persevered they would have opportunities ahead of them which their mothers had never had. She worked extremely hard, was paid as poorly as her teachers, but enjoyed the work enormously. She would return to this school twice more in later years and help it to develop into what is now Mary Leakey Girls' High School.

Fred, meanwhile, threw himself into the work of trying to build an essential foundation for the educational development of the country. The network of primary schools over this well-populated area of Kenya was very inadequate, although better than in many other areas. Many children didn't go to school at all, others went for a time and then dropped out because parents could not afford the low fees requested, facilities were minimal, many teachers were untrained and teaching salaries were very low.

Fred's work brought him into close contact with the local Kikuyu community. Having learned to speak Kikuyu and Kiswahili and having absorbed all they could about the traditions and life of the Kikuyu people around them, Fred and Eileen were aware of the ferment going on in the minds of many Kikuyu who wanted to drive the British out of their land. Between 1952 and 1956 there was a complex armed revolt led by the Kikuyu, the so-called 'Kenya Emergency', a rebellion against British rule and an attempt to re-establish traditional land rights. What they wanted was understandable, although the methods chosen by the Mau Mau organisers would bring great suffering to their own people. It gave Fred and Eileen their first taste of the political upheaval that was coming. They knew there would be change and many of those they had taught would be involved in it, for better or for worse. After the revolt, Britain gradually increased African representation in the colony's legislative council until in 1963 Kenya achieved independence, with Jomo Kenyatta as the first President.

Against the background of the Emergency, which caused enormous upset to Kikuyu life, Fred's work required a great deal of liaising with local communities and churches. He openly refused to carry a gun, although all white people were advised to do so by the police. He attributed the fact that he was never molested on his daily travels around the district to this stance, as he was not therefore a direct target for Mau Mau fighters. It would certainly have been very easy for them to ambush him if they had wanted to, as he was known to be visiting schools daily in his Land Rover on lonely roads. It is also possible that his work to increase the number of local community schools was seen as furthering the Mau Mau aim of African independence.

While Fred was Primary Schools Supervisor, Eileen enjoyed running two primary boarding schools for local girls. In 1955 she became Headmistress of Kikuyu Girls' School, started by the Church of Scotland, now the Musa Gitau School. Eileen enjoyed a close friendship with Mary Bruce, Headmistress of the neighbouring Alliance Girls' High School and it was her aim to have the best results in the country in the leaving examination from her primary school and to get as many girls as possible into Form 1 of Alliance Girls' High School. Girls from those two schools have remained her lifelong friends.

In 1959, after seven challenging years, Fred and Eileen moved into the expanding sphere of teacher training. They had lighter workloads than in their previous jobs and both put all their spare time into working for and obtaining theology degrees as external students of London University. They had become seriously interested in how religious education might be taught as a school subject and wanted a firm theological basis from which to start. They also did some postgraduate study in world religions and traditional African religions.

During this time, Eileen underwent a hysterectomy to remove a diseased uterus, meaning that she would never be able to have a child. Difficult though this was to accept, God showed her that she could find great fulfilment in her life as a teacher, and Fred was totally supportive in this, which meant a great deal. In 1961, when Fred accepted an assignment to visit and assess all the Protestant Theological and Bible training schools in Kenya, Uganda and Tanzania, Eileen returned as Headmistress of Kabete Girls' School, which had been selected for development into a new district secondary school.

In 1967 they moved back into Alliance High School where Fred was invited to teach the new A level courses which were being added. At the same time, Eileen was appointed to head up the religious education department at Kenya High School in Nairobi, the largest girls' school in the country, which fortunately was within commuting distance of Alliance High School, their home for the next twenty years.

They celebrated their silver wedding anniversary in 1973, travelling by coach from London to Kathmandu, stopping in a different location every night, experiencing many new countries and a wide variety of religious cultures. It was the journey of a lifetime, and took eleven weeks before they finally flew back across India to Kenya. In the following years they took any opportunity they could to travel to other African countries, to the USSR and the United States, always doing it as economically as possible, but revelling in their shared love of travel.

In 1974 Fred was accepted by the Anglican Church in Kenya for ordination to the chaplaincy of Alliance High School, as well as being in charge of religious education. By now the school had grown to a student body of six hundred, four times as large as it was in 1948 when Fred first joined the staff there.

One year later, Eileen was appointed Inspector of Christian Religious Education in the National Schools' Inspectorate, which entailed extensive travel, visiting schools and teacher training colleges across Kenya. As part of this role she ran courses across the country for RE teachers, many of whom had not had adequate training. She preferred to drive herself in her own car, sorting out accommodation as she went. She found Catholic convents the best place to stay and the Catholic sisters very welcoming. In 1979 she handed over to the first African Religious Education Inspector and returned to teaching A level RE, fitting it in with another aspect of her work in those years, the marking of examination papers for the Examinations Council. Getting standards right was an exacting task.

Throughout the seventies, Eileen was also involved in the production of a new Christian religious education syllabus for secondary schools, including the writing of three textbooks. In 1984 the schools' curriculum was totally changed by President Moi. Eileen was appointed to the panel responsible for writing a new syllabus and four more textbooks for the new system. It had to be done quickly and was exhausting work, especially as she could see the shortcomings of the changes.

By this stage, Fred and Eileen had seen the huge political and social shift take place from British colony to independent African republic. And of course they had come to love Kenya, the country which had become home to them. By the beginning of 1987 they had both reached the age of 63, and were well past the compulsory retirement age for government-paid teachers. The school which had been their home for the past twenty years was that same school, greatly expanded, to which they had first gone in 1948. It was not at all easy to see where or how to retire from such an active life. After almost forty years in Kenya, they did not feel they belonged in the UK any longer.

They had seen Kenya's political scene deteriorate in the 1980s in ways they did not like; the euphoria and optimism of the late 1960s and 1970s when 'nation-building' was the theme, was disappearing. Government policies were struggling to keep up with an uncontrolled population growth and the accompanying demands on the country's resources. Increasing discontent, resurgent tribalism, political repression and corruption became widespread, and random violence was a frequent news item. Kenya had seen its neighbour, Uganda, torn apart by civil war. Yet in all this, a voice of sanity often spoke out from the African churches whose membership, across all denominations, had greatly increased.

Fred was patron of the 'Theological Society' in the school, where sixth formers came in from other schools for discussion and debate; often there was an attendance of several hundred to hear the invited speaker and join in the popular discussions. At one such event in 1987, an 'old boy' of the school, by then a politician, presented his own views on Christianity and politics. It was reported in the government-controlled national newspaper as an attack on the government from a leading school. The Criminal Investigation Department descended on the school and interrogated Fred as patron of the Society, along with the Headmaster. The perceived threats were deportation for Fred and Eileen, removal of the Headmaster and possibly other staff, and unspecified action against the school.

Sadly, the Headmaster said to Fred and Eileen, 'We Kenyans can't get out of this. You can.' Fred and Eileen realised there was no alternative but to agree with him. Devastated, they felt their usefulness in Kenya had come to an end. As they packed up their belongings, they tried to prepare themselves mentally to leave friends, students, and the country that had become their home, where they had spent all their married life and where they had thought they would end their days.

Returning to England without a home of their own to go to
called for some creative thinking. Fred found a part-time position at a small Anglican church, offering accommodation in
return for church duties. It was well situated, in a rural area
close to beautiful countryside in the south of England. Eileen,
also licensed as a lay reader in the Anglican Church, assisted
Fred in the services he took and began to feel that maybe this
retirement situation was what they needed for their resettle-
ment back in Britain.

Gradually, however, Eileen became aware that all was not
well with Fred. He became easily depressed, worried about
what often seemed rather insignificant matters; he felt he was
slowing down and getting too tired. He seemed to benefit
from a prostatectomy and was given medication to control
hypertension, but an overall loss of confidence in his ability to
carry out the job he seemed to be doing very well was baffling.
The congregation welcomed and warmed to him and appreciated his ministry. In 1991, however, he decided to fully retire.

They found a small bungalow they could afford in a nearby
village and enjoyed several 'package' holidays to places they
had not visited before. Travel still excited them both and they
now had time to do it. As they settled into their village home,
they tried to have a daily walk, joined in the local church activities and made new friends. Fred began to take 'home communion' to housebound elderly people, was invited to take
occasional services in the village church and other churches in
the area, kept up a large correspondence with old friends and
read a great deal. Maybe they were finally adjusting to this
new phase of life and maybe his slowing down and fatigue
awareness were just an inevitable part of growing older.

Two years later, Eileen's seventieth birthday was marked by
an unexpected and unpleasant incident. On a quiet Sunday
morning while Fred was driving to church, he collided with
another car on a roundabout. Although neither driver suffered

obvious injury, Fred decided he was no longer a safe driver and never drove again from that day. He was obviously badly shaken and was relieved when Eileen agreed to do all the driving from then on.

In the winter of 1993, they made a return visit to Africa, staying with friends and revisiting Kenya as well as South Africa. Fred was glad to leave all the arrangements to Eileen, but was quite excited about the trip. Although they were given a very warm welcome, they noted with sadness that many of the overriding problems of the country still persisted. In the last week of their trip, they were invited to a surprise party held at a large sports club, where they were greeted by 150 'old boys' of Alliance High School, spanning the years 1948 to 1987. In true African fashion, each person shook hands with them individually and thanked them for being there. African food, Coca Cola and beer were plentiful, as were the speeches. The wonderful evening was summed up in the words on the card presented to them: 'For your selfless service and dedication to Alliance High School in particular and the country in general, we thank you. God bless you!' The occasion gave them great comfort and an abiding memory.

Although all went well, Fred clearly had to make much more effort than expected to keep going throughout the trip. On his return to England, it was obvious to Eileen that he was increasingly struggling to carry out his limited church duties effectively. Depressed and worried, he went to see his doctor, who referred him to the geriatrician at the local hospital.

Emerging from the consulting room, he said to Eileen, 'They checked everything in sight and they think I have early Parkinson's disease.' He was strangely relieved, feeling that there were worse things to have to deal with. Certainly his symptoms seemed to add up to a neurological brain dysfunction of some sort. They were advised to contact the Parkinson's Disease Society, learn as much as possible about dealing with the disease and accept that Fred would need to take daily medication for the rest of his life.

They began to work out their own strategies for positive living, for fighting this disease as long as they could. They decided to be open with other people about Fred's diagnosis, keep up as active a life as possible without putting Fred under pressure, continue going on holidays and seeing friends. They helped set up a local Parkinson's support group and Eileen arranged monthly social meetings which were well attended and much appreciated.

Fred found his hearing deteriorating and when the hearing aids available through the National Health Service did not seem to help, they went to some trouble and considerable expense to have one made privately for him. The unforeseen difficulty was that his fingers could not position it correctly into his ear and adjust its tiny controls. He resented having to ask Eileen to fit it for him. He also noticed his typing and handwriting were deteriorating and requiring more effort and concentration to avoid mistakes; brain and fingers seemed unwilling to co-operate, which was a source of increasing frustration.

But overall Eileen felt his medication and determination to live well with his condition were keeping things quite controlled. He enjoyed a daily walk, helped occasionally at church, and continued his home communion visits, with some assistance. They tried to maximise the good times, even moments, and had many good friends. They continued with their winter holidays, taking a hotel package to Cyprus at the beginning of 1995 and returning to South Africa and Kenya at the beginning of 1996.

In 1997 their winter holiday took them back to a very quiet stay with Eileen's South African cousin, planned as a reading holiday, as there was a good public library close to her home and her garden patio in the South African summer weather provided a very pleasant place for reading. But Eileen noticed that Fred's lifelong passion for reading seemed strangely blunted. He would choose interesting books to read but then find it difficult to get through them and afterwards not remember much about what he had read. He wanted to sleep much of the time, but still kept up an after-breakfast or early-evening walk when it was not too hot. He found the long air flight more tiring than ever before and, when they returned home, they decided reluctantly that it had to be their last visit to Africa.

The year 1998 marked an important milestone in their life together, as they reached their golden wedding anniversary. They were both deeply happy to have achieved fifty years together, to have kept those vows made on their wedding day and to have shared so much along the way. They both wanted to have a celebration and good friends made it possible to hold an informal party at the church on their anniversary date. A splendid buffet supper was organised, to which 90 friends and neighbours were invited. A photographic record of their lives was put on display and made a good talking point for the guests. No one who came had actually known them before 1989, when they first moved to that part of England, so what they had done before that was of some interest and speculation. That evening, which left them both wonderfully aware of still being in love, was a beautiful climax of their shared life which, sadly, from then on was to be an increasing battle against irreversible illness.

On one of their daily walks together, not long after the anniversary party, Fred started to see other strange, imaginary people around them, and became confused and worried about who Eileen really was. He wanted to talk about it, to try to find some explanation for the invasion of their lives by these strange people and Eileen struggled to explain that, although he saw these people, she did not. For the time being he accepted this, though uneasily. The fact that Eileen couldn't see them didn't prove they didn't exist, but Fred decided to call them the 'unreal' people, which at least covered their differing perceptions of them.

On the doctor's advice, they decided to proceed with their usual winter holiday in January 1999. Even if the 'unreal' people insisted on coming with them, it seemed better to go into Spain's winter sunshine than to stay in cold and wet England. Fred remained very fatigued but on bright mornings they were able to go out for walks around the hotel, which he enjoyed. While they were out, he would talk quite sensibly and happily but on their return he would be confused about where he was, or who Eileen was, and what they were doing there. He enjoyed going out for a good Spanish meal but by the evening would have forgotten what they had done. He had lost weight and his awareness of his mental difficulties troubled him. His concentration fluctuated and occasional incontinence caused problems.

He was tolerant of accepting help from Eileen with bathing routines, which he admitted he was finding more of a nuisance to cope with. She made sure his medication was taken at the right times and they spent a lot of time just talking, which he wanted to do. He asked many questions about their earlier life, much of which he seemed to be forgetting. He tried reading aloud to Eileen, thinking it would help him to speak more clearly, but it didn't, which worried him. He enjoyed the small informal Sunday service held in the hotel but told Eileen that he was finding his daily prayers and Bible reading difficult 'because the words don't make sense'. They tried doing that together, which helped a little.

Eileen felt that above all she had to be reassuring to him. She could see no point in abandoning their holiday because of Fred's deterioration. She hoped he might settle down and adjust. He was enjoying gentle walking in the very attractive area around the hotel, he was eating quite well and a friend living nearby was prepared to help if they needed it. The Spanish winter was a great improvement on what was on offer in Britain.

On their return home, Eileen knew she had to see the doctor as soon as possible. She was finding it increasingly difficult to cope with the unpredictable fluctuations in Fred's mental state and the accompanying distress he was obviously experiencing. Something else seemed to be going on as well as Parkinson's disease. He was becoming more and more dependent on Eileen to keep him going from day to day and his determination to 'live well' in spite of Parkinson's was faltering painfully.

In early June they had a visit from a psychogeriatrician, specialising in mental illness in the elderly. For an hour he encouraged Fred to talk and to attempt various perception and memory tests. He then talked to Eileen on her own, explaining that the most probable diagnosis was dementia with Lewy bodies, which produces symptoms seen in both Parkinson's and Alzheimer's disease. Microscopic deposits or 'bodies' develop and destroy nerve cells in the brain. The condition, which is progressive and incurable, is named after Dr Lewy who first wrote about it. Knowing that Fred would want to know, Eileen asked the doctor to explain it to him. He seemed to accept what he was told. He understood that he was becoming increasingly ill and wanted some explanation. How to face this illness was something they still had to deal with.

The doctor outlined some coping strategies. A community psychiatric nurse would visit them regularly at home, there would be regular checks on Fred's condition, and a recent drug called Aricept, found to be helpful to some dementia patients, would be prescribed.

Eileen joined the Alzheimer's Society and obtained all the information available on the care of dementia patients. She was also advised to watch her own health. She obtained an 'enduring power of attorney' to secure her legal position in handling their finances. The sense that others were now helping her care for Fred was like a ray of light in increasing darkness. 'I was indescribably saddened by what I saw was happening to Fred but I was helped to go on because I no longer felt directionless.'

Throughout the rest of that year, enjoyable short walks, occasional good conversation and happy time spent with friends were interspersed with the frustration, confusion, incoherence, disorientation and depression which could descend suddenly like a dark cloud. At times Fred would get irritated and argue angrily with Eileen, who tried hard not to confront or become personally annoyed, but rather to calm or distract him. It was not easy. One evening, when Eileen suggested he change his clothes after washing, he burst out, 'I'm tired of this place! I must get away from here! I don't want to be treated like a baby and told what to do!'

Often, however, he wanted her spoken reassurance that she still loved him and he was comforted if they just sat together with her arm around him. They still shared a double bed, which he wanted, although there were occasional times when he wasn't sure if she was really his wife or one of those 'unreal' people who still appeared and disappeared and worried him.

When he knew that he was confused or frustrated, he often apologised to her for being such a nuisance. Eileen tried to take an objective view. 'I decided that the best way to respond to that was to say that he would never be a nuisance to me, but his illness was a great nuisance to us both.' The idea of the illness being the real nuisance or even his 'enemy' that they had to try to overcome seemed to help him. They agreed that what was happening to him was certainly a form of evil and not some kind of punishment from God. Fred was trying to hold on to his belief in a loving God and Eileen did all she could to uphold that faith. There was a significant spiritual aspect of 'caring' that wasn't spelt out in the medical research papers on DLB or the literature on the practicalities of dementia care.

Eileen herself needed to hang on to her faith in a God of love who would carry them through this 'valley of the shadow of death'.

'As I learned more about Fred's brain disease and its effects, I knew his death in the foreseeable future was inevitable and I had to try to prepare him and myself for that. The teaching of the New Testament on the reality of the spiritual dimension of life on resurrection into God's eternal life became increasingly significant to me. Inevitably, at the end of life as we know it now, the physical body, including the brain, wears out and is of no further use, like worn-out and discarded clothes. But beyond time and space and all the limitations of our human life is the reality of spiritual life in God, exciting, wonderful and beyond our imagination now. That faith was what I had to try to sustain in Fred's consciousness and mine.'

Eileen made no secret of Fred's increasing illness and was greatly encouraged by the positive response of many of their friends. She was aware of the widespread social stigma connected with mental illness, especially when accompanied by socially inappropriate behaviour. The support and love of those who still saw the real person in Fred, and not just another sad dementia case, carried her through the darkest days.

Fred began taking Aricept in August and his encouraging response to the medication made them both think that perhaps they might still have another winter holiday. The doctors were supportive but warned that this would probably be their last holiday together, as there was little likelihood that Fred would be able to have any further holidays because of anticipated deterioration ahead. Aware that she needed to choose very carefully which place might best suit Fred's needs, Eileen booked six weeks in Cyprus during January and February, at a hotel where a Christian organisation was running holidays.

It went as well as they could have hoped. Inevitably Fred's difficulties went with them but he survived the travel, adjusted reasonably well to the hotel and enjoyed the company of a number of fellow guests who were friendly and accepting of his needs when they were told about them. To their pleasant surprise, they met several ex-Kenya acquaintances as well as making some new friends. The weather was generally kind and they had some pleasant walks. Eileen did everything she could to help him feel relaxed and unpressurised and had come fully prepared for every eventuality, including the increasing incontinence. Every evening she helped him with washing and undressing, which he was now glad for her to do. She was very glad they had that special holiday together. It gave her a break, which she needed, and gave Fred some happiness.

A month after arriving back in England, Fred caught a cold which developed into a chest infection. All the dementia symptoms worsened, putting increased strain on Eileen as she tried to care for him. The consultant arranged for Fred to have a period of continuous assessment for two weeks in a newly-opened hospital unit not far from their home. Having visited the unit, Eileen, impressed with what she saw, decided to take the opportunity to spend the first week of Fred's time there with her brother, to unwind a little and get some nights of unbroken sleep. Her normal sleep pattern was totally disrupted because of Fred's restlessness and disorientation at night and she was permanently tired. While she was away, two kind friends agreed to call in to see Fred each day.

On her return, however, she was disturbed to find Fred very distressed and confused, totally bewildered at her absence, thinking she was dead or had abandoned him. He had no memory of her explaining why he was being admitted to the unit and was worried that he could not leave. Once he recognised her again, he just held on to her like a dependent child whose world was falling to pieces. 'In his mind I was the only one who could help him stick the pieces together and make sense of everything, but I knew I had to have help to keep going. I couldn't carry on the struggle single-handed.'

At the end of his stay in hospital, a rota of carers was organised to come in and help Fred prepare for bed each evening and a day 'companion' came for four hours each week to give Eileen some free time. Fred was also taken to a day centre once a week. These arrangements took some of the pressure off Eileen, especially as Fred liked the carers who came. The day centre was not so successful, the only positive thing for him being lunch – because he went on a Friday, it was usually his favourite fish and chips.

The permanently disturbed nights, however, were an ongoing problem. Fred had been prescribed mild sleeping pills which did not seem to help much. By the end of each day he was always very tired and his physical symptoms worse, affecting his ability to get in and out of bed. After some initial sleep, he would wake and struggle out of bed, at increasing risk of falling. Although hand rails had been put up to help him, when he got up in the night he seemed oblivious to everything except the desire to try to move around aimlessly. He would struggle from window to door, door to door, cupboard to cupboard, room to room. He was like a sleepwalker, unresponsive to what Eileen said to him and the only way for her to deal with it was to get up herself to watch that he was safe and wait till he wandered back to bed. Having been helped back into bed and back to sleep again for a while, he would then wake and struggle up again.

The effect on Eileen of having to try to handle this pattern was one of steadily increasing tiredness. She made arrangements for the day care facility to be replaced by a couple of nights away each week in a nearby private residential care home, in order to give her a regular chance to sleep properly and build up her own reserves to get through the other nights without breaking down. Fred did not find it easy to accept and the staff of the home did not find him the easiest person to deal with, but it was the best they could do if Eileen was to continue caring for him at home much longer.

In spite of all their coping strategies, there was an overall worsening in Fred's condition. He could no longer write, could hardly read, and his short-term memory was much worse. He could not concentrate on talking books or the radio or television. There was still the unpredictable fluctuation in his mental state that had been noticeable for so long. Sometimes he still wanted to go for a walk or a drive in the car. He still struggled to get to church for a Sunday service, although he tended to doze through most of it. He enjoyed visits from friends who did not make him feel pressurised, and he and Eileen still sat and talked together. Sometimes they browsed through photograph albums, and Eileen would remind him what the photos were about.

She was advised that by the following year she would almost certainly not be able to look after him, as the predicted decline into total dementia would require full-time care beyond her strength and abilities. She knew that this was realistic advice and so began the depressing task of finding out which homes in the area would accept dementia patients. She was moving from coping strategies to survival tactics and suddenly she felt a lot older than her 77 years. What it was like in Fred's tormented world, she could only guess.

On 24 November 2000, Fred was very tired and depressed. Very clearly he said to Eileen, 'I feel so bad, I want to commit suicide. I've had enough. I want to die.'

Eileen struggled to find a helpful answer.

'Your illness is extremely hard to live with. God knows when you will die, and it will be a wonderful release into God's loving presence from what you are suffering now. Do you remember how Mother Teresa described dying? She said it was "going home to God".' Fred seemed comforted, taking the point that suicide was not really an easy option, but there was no doubt in Eileen's mind about the very deep distress that he felt and the suffering caused by his increasing deterioration.

On 23 December, his seventy-seventh birthday, Eileen had invited several friends for cake and tea in the afternoon. During the night of the 22nd, he was unwell, restless and feverish; the next morning, he collapsed into near-unconsciousness. The doctor who was called diagnosed pneumonia and admitted him once again to the hospital he had been in before, where he was put on antibiotics and a drip, but taken off Aricept, the drug that had probably controlled some of the mental deterioration. Physically he was very weak and helpless and his mental state rapidly grew worse.

Eileen visited him every day and was grateful to other friends who went to see him. The care he was given was good, the consultant and community psychiatric nurse understanding and supportive, encouraging Eileen to talk freely with them about his condition. She knew he was approaching the final phase of his life and asked for him not to be resuscitated if he had another crisis. 'I couldn't see any point in trying to keep his exhausted body functioning beyond its natural strength at this stage of his life. Long before this he had made it clear to me that he was as ready to die as it was possible for him to be, as a Christian believer. To ignore that and try to intervene would be to come between him and "going home to God".'

Although Fred was usually drowsy and unresponsive, and incoherent if he tried to talk, there were other moments when some recognition and lucidity returned. There were times when he wanted to know where he was and why he was there, but Eileen's explanation that he had been very ill and was being looked after in hospital seemed to satisfy him. She fed him drinks and the liquidised food which was all he could now swallow, taking a little pressure off the care staff.

She continued to talk to him or just sit by him if he was asleep. It was a great help that he had been given a room to himself.

'In the times when he surely knew me, I told him how much I loved him and put my arm around him, and several times he whispered his own endearments to me. On 15 January, when I had talked to him a little, he asked me quite clearly, "When can I die?" After that, each day I asked God the same question for Fred, praying for his mercy on us both.'

The disease up-ended their lives, but could not destroy the love and fulfilment they had had. In a rare and brief moment of lucidity in what proved to be the final week of his life, Fred whispered to her, 'You're a lovely girl,' and she answered, 'You're my darling sweetheart.' They were both 77 years old and had been married for 52 years.

When Fred died a few days later, on 19 February 2001, Eileen felt a strange relief and peace, together with awareness of very deep loss. At last Fred was freed from his tormenting struggle against dementia and she found she could thank God for the gift of love she had received in the life Fred and she had shared. Fred himself, she had no doubt, had 'gone home to God' and that gave her the strength she needed to move on into what was left of her own journey.

Following his wishes, Fred's ashes were taken to Kenya and buried in the grounds of Alliance Boys' High School, in a little graveyard near the chapel, alongside his friend Carey Francis. It is fitting that his grave should be there, in the midst of the school and the Kikuyu countryside he loved so much. On the simple headstone of Kenyan marble is a brief text from 1 John 4:16, 'God is Love'.

Eileen was very clear about that Bible verse on the headstone. 'We can't describe God. The more we get to know him, the more we realise that love is the purest description of him we have. It was a very significant verse for both of us.'

When she revisited Kenya after Fred's death, it gave Eileen great pleasure to meet up again with past students and colleagues, who welcomed her with great affection and shared with her the stories of their lives. As she saw these confident, mature and lovely middle-aged women who had once been in her care as young girls facing an unknown future, she realised how worthwhile it had all been. She looked on them now as her adopted daughters; they were her legacy to Kenya.

Eileen revisited Alliance High School three times between 2001 and 2004, well over fifty years after she first arrived there, aged just 25. Together she and Fred had followed their dream, lived the adventure and known God's strength in all the twists of the path. When the time comes, her ashes will be buried in Kenya beside Fred's, in that place to which they devoted so much of their life.

She reflects, 'Neither of us was the perfect partner, we were taking on each other just as we were; there were rough patches and finally Fred's dementia, but at the end Fred could still call me "a lovely girl" and I could call him "my darling sweetheart" and mean it. Our first love grew over the years into something enduring and very beautiful, lasting beyond illness and death – a tiny reflection of God's love for us.'

God is love.
1 John 4:16

Endnotes

1. Connie Kasari and Connie Wong, 'Five Early Signs of Autism', *The Exceptional Parent* (Nov 2002). http://findarticles.com/p/articles/mi_go2827/is_11_32/ai_n7288958/?tag=content;col1.
2. *Shadowlands* (UK, Paramount Pictures, 1993).
3. William and Sharyn McKay, *The Voice of Hope* (Belfast: Ambassador Productions, 2006).
4. www.oldwarrenpointforum.com.
5. Kerry and Chris Shook, *One Month to Live* (Colorado Springs: Random House Inc., 2008).
6. http://bjc.oxfordjournals.org/cgi/pdf_extract/30/4/525.
7. http://www.gravematters.org.uk/epitaph-text.htm.
8. http://www.special-dictionary.com/proverbs/source/p/persian_proverb/15.htm.
9. Genesis 2:24.
10. http://truefreedomtrust.co.uk/basis.html.

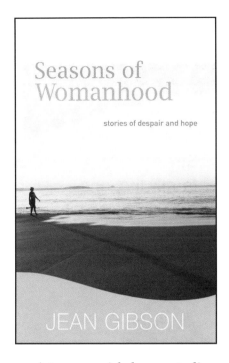

Seasons of Womanhood

Jean Gibson

- A teenage girl chooses to live with a well-known paramilitary figure in Belfast, Northern Ireland.
- A young teacher works through the issue of singleness, facing up to the fact that she will probably never marry.
- A wife suffers seventeen years of hurt and pain as her husband fights against her love for God.
- A prominent singer is devastated when she learns that it is medically impossible for her to have a child.

Seasons of Womanhood is a contemporary collection of these and other inspiring stories from women who have faced the reality of life and proved the sufficiency of God's power in many different situations. It covers various stages of a woman's life, from early days through to the final years. Jean Gibson clearly shows us that none of us is alone in our experience and that no situation is beyond hope.

978-1-86024-627-2 ● **£5.99**

Care for the Family

Strengthening family life, and helping those who are hurting due to family breakdown.

Visit www.careforthefamily.org.uk to find out more or phone (029) 2081 0800